POCKET

T0023684

FRENCH PHRASES

FOR BEGINNERS

GAIL STEIN

Publisher Mike Sanders
Editor Christopher Stolle
Designer William Thomas
Compositor Ayanna Lacey
Technical Editor Madeleine Vasaly
Proofreader Madeleine Vasaly
Indexer Beverlee Day

First American Edition, 2022
Published in the United States by DK Publishing
6081 E. 82nd Street, Indianapolis, Indiana 46250

Copyright © 2022 by Gail Stein
22 23 24 25 26   10 9 8 7 6 5 4 3 2 1
001-326986-MAR2022

Published in the United States by Dorling Kindersley Limited.

ISBN: 978-0-7440-5143-8
Library of Congress Catalog Number: 2021944232

Note: This publication contains the opinions and ideas of its authors.
It is intended to provide helpful and informative material on the subject
matter covered. It is sold with the understanding that the author(s) and
publisher are not engaged in rendering professional services in the book.
If the reader requires personal assistance or advice, a competent
professional should be consulted. The authors and publisher specifically
disclaim any responsibility for any liability, loss, or risk, personal
or otherwise, which is incurred as a consequence, directly or indirectly,
of the use and application of any of the contents of this book.

Trademarks: All terms mentioned in this book that are known
to be or are suspected of being trademarks or service marks
have been appropriately capitalized. Alpha Books, DK, and Penguin
Random House LLC cannot attest to the accuracy of this information.
Use of a term in this book should not be regarded as affecting
the validity of any trademark or service mark.

DK books are available at special discounts when
purchased in bulk for sales promotions, premiums, fund-raising,
or educational use. For details, contact SpecialSales@dk.com.

Printed and bound in the United States

All images © Dorling Kindersley Limited
For further information see: www.dkimages.com

For the curious
www.dk.com

Contents

Dedication

This book is dedicated to my adorable Stein grandchildren: Francesca, Theresa, and Julian. Special thanks to my incredibly supportive editor, Christopher Stolle.

Introduction

In today's fast-growing, ever-expanding multicultural world, the acquisition of a foreign language is a must for travel, business, and other pursuits. Learning French will allow you to enter a world of endless opportunities, intriguing experiences, and exciting challenges. It will provide you with the key that opens the door to a different lifestyle, a distinctive culture, and a unique, romantic outlook on life. It will give you a valuable tool that will serve you well—whether you're heading to a French-speaking country or to your local boutique.

What's Inside

You'll learn pronunciation and grammar painlessly and effortlessly without sacrificing speed and accuracy. Whether you're a student, a traveler, or a businessperson, this book will teach you the basics while giving you the vocabulary and the phrases you'll find most useful in almost every conceivable daily situation. You'll be introduced to a wide variety of topics: food, clothing, sports, health, social media, and much more.

This book isn't merely a phrase book, a grammar text, or a travel companion—it's a combination. That makes it not only unique but also an extremely useful tool for people who want a working command of French. It will allow you to understand and to be understood without embarrassment or frustration and with ease and enjoyment. Yes, learning French can be fun!

This book was written with you in mind. That's why it's so user-friendly. By the time you've read through it, you'll be a pro at ordering a meal to suit your diet, watching a French film without completely depending on the subtitles, meeting new friends, dealing with security personnel before they perform a full-body search at the airport, getting the biggest bang for your buck, and getting help in an emergency. You'll be amazed and surprised at how rapidly you'll learn what you need to know.

Chapter 1

Quick Pronunciation Guide

Although French sounds are different from those in English, with practice and patience, you should master them without too much difficulty.

Stress

In French, each syllable of a word has almost equal stress. When speaking French, pronounce each syllable with equal emphasis, except for the last syllable of a group of words, which should get a slightly stronger emphasis.

Diacritical Marks

Mark	Significance	Examples
´ (acute accent)	Used only on an *e* (*é*) to produce the sound *ay* as in *day*	*bébé* bay-bay
` (grave accent)	Used on an *a* (*à*): no sound change; *e* (*è*): produces the sound *eh*, as in *met*; or *u* (*ù*): no sound change	*à* ah *très* treh *où* oo
^ (circumflex accent)	Used on all vowels: *â, ê, î, ô, û*; longer vowel sounds for *â* and *ô*; slightly longer vowel sound for *ê*; almost imperceptible for *î* and *û*	*pâte* paht *fête* feht *île* eel *hôtel* o-tehl *sûr* sewr

| , (cedilla) | Used only on a c (ç) before *a*, *o*, or *u* to produce a soft *c* (the sound of *s*) | *ça* sah *garçon* gahr-sohN *reçu* ruh-sew |
| ¨ (dieresis) | Used on the second vowel in a series; each vowel pronounced separately | *Noël* noh-ehl *Haïti* ah-ee-tee |

To learn how to pronounce nasal sounds (like that in *garçon*), see page 6.

The letter *é* often replaces an *s* from older French: *étranger* (stranger). Adding a mental *s* after ^ plus a vowel can help determine meaning: *île* (isle).

Vowels

Vowel	Pronunciation	Examples
a	*ah*	*la* lah
à		*à* ah
â		*château* shah-toh

continues

Vowel	Pronunciation	Examples
é	*ay*	*café* kah-fay
final *er* or final *ert*		*aider* ay-day
ez		*chez* shay
e (in one-syllable words or in the middle of a word followed by a single consonant)	*uh*	*le* luh *premier* pruh-myay
è	*eh*	*très* treh
ê		*fête* feht
e (plus two consonants or a final pronounced consonant)		*sept* seht *billet* bee-yeh
et		*seize* sehz
ei		*mai* meh
ai		*aider* ay-day
i	*ee*	*il* eel
î		*île* eel

o (before *se*)	*o*	*rose* roz
o (last pronounced sound of a word)		*sabot* sah-bo
ô		*allô* ah-lo
au		*au* o
eau		*bureau* bew-ro
o (when followed by a pronounced consonant)	*oh* (like in *love*)	*homme* ohm
ou	*oo*	*ou* oo
où		*sou* soo
oû		*goût* goo
oi	*wah*	*oiseau* wah-zo
oy		*soyez* swah-yay
u	*ew*	*tu* tew
û		*sûr* sewr

The *i* + *ll* combination is usually a *y* sound, except in *mille* (meel), *million* (mee-lyohN), *tranquille* (trahN-keel), *village* (vee-lahzh), and *ville* (veel). (See page 6 for more on nasal [N] sounds.)

Nasals

Nasal sounds occur when a vowel is followed by a single *n* or *me* in the same syllable. In the pronunciations in this book, you'll see a vowel sound followed by *N*. This indicates you must make a nasal sound.

French Nasal	Symbol	Pronunciation	Examples
an (*am*)	ahN	Similar to *on* but with little emphasis on *n*	*an* ahN
en (*em*)			*chambre* shahNbr
			en ahN
			embarras ahN-bah-rah
in (*im*)	aN	Similar to *an* but with little emphasis on *n*	*incident* aN-see-dahN
ain (*aim*)			*impur* aN-pewr
			ainsi aN-see
			faim faN
oin	waN	Similar to *wa* (like in *wag*)	*loin* lwaN
ien	yaN	Similar to *yan* (like in *Yankee*)	*bien* byaN
on (*om*)	ohN	Similar to *on* (like in *long*)	*on* ohN
un (*um*)	uhN	Similar to *un* (like in *under*)	*un* uhN

Consonants

Most final consonants aren't pronounced except for
c, *r*, *f*, and *l*. The final *s* isn't pronounced in French.

Letter	Pronunciation	Examples
b, d, f, k, l, m, n, p, s, t, v, z	Same as English	*belle* behl
		film feelm
		mère mehr
		salaire sah-lehr
		zéro zay-ro
c (hard sound before *a, o, u,* or a consonant)	*k*	*carte* kahrt
		code kohd
qu		*cure* kewr
final *q*		*qui* kee
		cinq saNk

continues

Letter	Pronunciation	Example
c (soft sound before *e*, *i*, *y*)	s	*ce* suh
ç		*ici* ee-see
		bicyclette bee-see-kleht
		ça sah
ch	sh	*chanson* shahN-sohN
g (hard sound before *a*, *o*, *u*, or a consonant)	g (as in *good*)	*gai* geh
		golf gohlf
gu (before *e*, *i*, *y*)		*guitare* gee-tahr
		grec grehk
		guerre gehr
		guide geed
		Guy gee

Letter	Pronunciation	Example
g (soft sound before *e*, *i*, *y*)	*zh* (like the *s* in *pleasure*)	*âge* ahzh
ge (soft sound before *a*, *o*)		*girafe* zhee-rahf
		gym zheem
		mangeais mahN-zheh
		mangeons mahN-zhohN
gn	*ny* (like the *ni* in *union*)	*oignon* oh-nyohN
h	always silent (see page 10)	*hôpital* o-pee-tahl
j	*zh*	*je* zhuh
r	*r* (see page 10)	*race* rahs
s at the beginning of a word	*s*	*sa* sah
s next to a consonant		*bistro* bees-tro
s between vowels	*z*	*maison* meh-zohN
-sion		*vision* vee-zyohN
th	*t*	*thé* tay
x + consonant	*ks*	*expert* ehks-pehr
x + vowel	*gz*	*exact* ehgz-ahkt

continues

Letter	Pronunciation	Examples
x (in these words only)	*s*	*six* sees
		dix dees
		soixante swah-sahNt

The letter *h* is usually used as a vowel and therefore requires elision with a vowel (see below) that might precede it: *l'homme* (lohm; the man). Other times, *h* is used as a consonant and doesn't require elision with the preceding vowel: *le héros* (luh ay-ro; the hero). Consult a dictionary for specifics.

The French *r* is pronounced at the back of the throat with the tongue resting at the bottom of the mouth against the teeth.

Liaison & Elision

Liaison is the linking of the final consonant of one word with the beginning vowel of the next word.

> *Vous arrivez.*
> voo zah-ree-vay

Elision is when there are two pronounced vowel sounds: one at the end of a word and the other at the beginning of the next word. The first vowel is dropped and replaced by an apostrophe.

> *Je + arrive = J'arrive*
> *le + hôtel = l'hôtel*

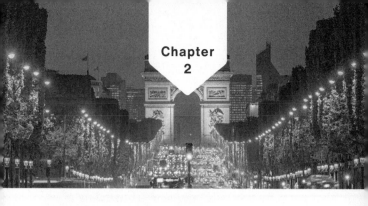

French You Already Know

You might not realize it, but our everyday
vocabulary is filled with many French words
and phrases. Café, restaurant, amateur, boutique,
bureau, chauffeur, depot, entrepreneur, fiancé and
fiancée, genre, and souvenir are just some examples
of words the English language has borrowed from
the French. The lists on the following pages give
you even more easily recognizable words.

Cognates

A *cognate* is a foreign word that's spelled exactly the same or almost the same as a word in English and has the same meaning. English has sometimes borrowed French words (letter for letter) and has incorporated them into our own vocabulary. Cognates are generally pronounced differently in each language, but the meaning of the French word is quite obvious to anyone who speaks English.

The following lists of nouns and adjectives provide you with cognates you might find useful. Keep these gender rules in mind:

- Nouns preceded by *le* are masculine singular.

- Nouns preceded by *la* are feminine singular.

- Nouns beginning with a vowel and preceded by *l'* might be masculine or feminine. They must be memorized.

- Adjectives ending in *-e* can be either masculine or feminine.

- Most masculine adjectives ending in a consonant can be made feminine by adding *-e*.

Exact Cognates

Masculine Nouns

le ballet	luh bah-leh
le chef	luh shehf
le client	luh klee-yahN
le concert	luh kohN-sehr

le dossier	luh do-syay
le film	luh feelm
le fruit	luh frwee
le hamburger	luh ahN-boor-guhr
le journal	luh zhoor-nahl
le massage	luh mah-sahzh
le menu	luh muh-new
le rendez-vous	luh rahN-day-voo
le restaurant	luh rehs-toh-rahN
le sport	luh spohr
le train	luh traN

Feminine Nouns

la brunette	lah brew-neht
la date	lah daht
la dispute	lah dees-pewt
la gazette	lah gah-zeht
la machine	lah mah-sheen
la note	lah noht
la page	lah pahzh
la photo	lah foh-to
la phrase	lah frahz
la question	lah kehs-tyohN
la statue	lah stah-tew
la table	lah tahbl
la technique	lah tehk-neek
le vinaigrette	luh vee-neh-greht

Nouns Beginning with a Vowel

l'accident (m.)	lahk-see-dahN
l'album (m.)	lahl-buhm
l'animal (m.)	lah-nee-mahl
l'automobile (f.)	loh-toh-moh-beel
l'avenue (f.)	lahv-new
l'olive (f.)	loh-leev
l'omelette (f.)	lohm-leht
l'orange (f.)	loh-rahnzh

Adjectives

blond	blohN
certain	sehr-taN
content	kohN-tahN
excellent	ehks-eh-lahN
horrible	oh-reebl
immense	ee-mahNs
important	aN-pohr-tahN
intelligent	aN-teh-lee-zhahN
patient	pah-syahN
sociable	soh-syahbl
unique	ew-neek

Almost Exact Cognates

These words, which are nearly the same in French and English, are easily recognizable.

Masculine Nouns

le dentiste	luh dahN-teest
le diamant	luh dee-ah-mahN
le docteur	luh dohk-tuhr
le jardin	luh zhahr-daN
le parc	luh pahrk
le professeur	luh proh-feh-suhr
le programme	luh proh-grahm
le supermarché	luh sew-pehr-mahr-shay
le téléphone	luh tay-lay-fohn
le théâtre	luh tay-ahtr
le touriste	luh too-reest
le vendeur	luh vahN-duhr

Feminine Nouns

la carotte	lah kah-roht
la cathédrale	lah kah-tay-drahl
la chambre	lah shahNbr
la classe	lah klahs
la couleur	lah koo-luhr
la danse	lah dahNs
la famille	lah fah-mee-y
la fontaine	lah fohN-tehn
la lampe	lah lahNp
la lettre	lah lehtr
la musique	lah mew-zeek

continues

la personne	lah pehr-sohn
la salade	lah sah-lahd
la soupe	lah soop
la tomate	lah toh-maht

Nouns Beginning with a Vowel

l'agence (f.)	lah-zhahNs
l'anniversaire (m.)	lah-nee-vehr-sehr
l'appartement (m.)	lah-pahr-tuh-mahN
l'artiste (m./f.)	lahr-teest
l'employé (m.)	lahN-plwah-yay
l'enfant (m./f.)	lahN-fahN
l'histoire (f.)	lees-twahr
l'hôtel (m.)	lo-tehl
l'objet (m.)	lohb-zheh
l'oncle (m.)	lohNkl
l'orchestre (m.)	lohr-kehstr

Adjectives

confortable	kohN-fohr-tahbl
amusant	ah-mew-zahN
difficile	dee-fee-seel
élégant	ay-lay-gahN
intéressant	aN-tay-reh-sahN
moderne	moh-dehrn
populaire	poh-pew-lehr
rapide	rah-peed
sincère	saN-sehr
splendide	splahN-deed
superbe	sew-pehrb

Verbs

Verbs (action words) can also be cognates. Most
French verbs fall into one of three categories:

- The -er family

- The -ir family

- The -re family

These are considered regular because all verbs within
the families have the same rules of conjugation.

-er Verb Cognates

accompagner	ah-kohN-pah-nyay
adorer	ah-doh-ray
aider	ay-day
blâmer	blah-may
changer	shahN-zhay
chanter	shahN-tay
commander	koh-mahN-day
commencer	koh-mahN-say
danser	dahN-say
décider	day-see-day
demander	duh-mahN-day
désirer	day-zee-ray
dîner	dee-nay
échanger	ay-shahN-zhay
embrasser	ahN-brah-say
entrer	ahN-tray
hésiter	ay-zee-tay
ignorer	ee-nyoh-ray

continues

inviter	aN-vee-tay
juger	zhoo-zhay
marcher	mahr-shay
observer	ohp-sehr-vay
pardonner	pahr-doh-nay
passer	pah-say
payer	pay-yay
persuader	pehr-swah-day
porter	pohr-tay
préparer	pray-pah-ray
présenter	pray-zahN-tay
prouver	proo-vay
recommander	ruh-koh-mahN-day
refuser	ruh-few-zay
regarder	ruh-gahr-day
regretter	ruh-greh-tay
remarquer	ruh-mahr-kay
réparer	ray-pah-ray
réserver	ray-zehr-vay
signer	see-nyay
tourner	toor-nay
vérifier	vay-ree-fyay

-ir Verb Cognates

accomplir	ah-kohN-pleer
applaudir	ah-plo-deer
finir	fee-neer

-re Verb Cognates

défendre	day-fahNdr
répondre	ray-pohNdr
vendre	vahNdr

False Friends (*Faux Amis*)

Faux amis (fo zah-mee) are words spelled exactly the same or almost the same in French and English but that have very different meanings in each language and might even be different parts of speech.

French	English Meaning
actuellement ahk-tew-ehl-mahN	currently
attendre ah-tahNdr	to wait
blesser bleh-say	to wound
le bras luh brah	arm
car kahr	because
le coin luh kwaN	corner
comment koh-mahN	how
crier kree-yay	to scream
la figure lah fee-gewr	face
l'habit lah-bee	item of clothing
introduire aN-troh-dweer	to insert
joli zhoh-lee	pretty
la journée lah zhoor-nay	day
large lahrzh	wide
la librairie lah lee-breh-ree	bookstore

continues

le livre luh leevr	book
la location lah loh-kah-syohN	rental
l'occasion loh-kah-zyohN	opportunity
le pain luh paN	bread
la pièce lah pyehs	coin or room
le préservatif luh pray-sehr-vah-teef	condom
la prune lah prewn	plum
le raisin luh reh-zaN	grape
rester rehs-tay	to remain
sale sahl	dirty
le sang luh sahN	blood
sensible sahN-seebl	sensitive
le stage luh stahzh	internship
le store luh stohr	window shade
travailler trah-vah-yay	to work

Idioms

An idiom is a phrase or expression whose meaning
can't be readily understood by either its grammar
or the words used to express it. Although idioms
might seem illogical, they allow you to speak and
express yourself in a foreign language the way
a native speaker would.

With Verbs

Some idioms are formed with verbs. To use them, simply conjugate the verb to agree with the subject. Make sure you put the verb in the proper tense (past, present, future).

apprendre par cœur ah-prahNdr pahr kuhr	to memorize
avoir … ans ah-vwahr … ahN	to be … years old
avoir besoin de ah-vwahr buh-zwaN duh	to need
avoir chaud ah-vwahr sho	to be warm
avoir de la chance ah-vwahr duh lah shahNs	to be lucky
avoir envie de (+ infinitive) ah-vwahr ahN-vee duh	to feel like (doing)
avoir faim ah-vwahr faN	to be hungry
avoir froid ah-vwahr frwah	to be cold
avoir l'habitude de (+ infinitive) ah-vwahr lah-bee-tewd duh	to be accustomed to
avoir l'intention de ah-vwahr laN-tahN-syohN duh	to intend to
avoir l'occasion de (+ infinitive) ah-vwahr loh-kah-zyohN duh	to have the opportunity to
avoir le temps de (+ infinitive) ah-vwahr luh tahN duh	to have (the) time to
avoir lieu ah-vwahr lyuh	to take place
avoir mal (à) (+ body part) ah-vwahr mahl (ah)	to have a pain (in)

avoir peur (de) ah-vwahr puhr (duh)	to be afraid of
avoir raison ah-vwahr reh-zohN	to be right
avoir soif ah-vwahr swahf	to be thirsty
avoir tort ah-vwahr tohr	to be wrong
donner sur doh-nay sewr	to face, look out on
être à ehtr ah	to belong to
être d'accord (avec) ehtr dah-kohr (ah-vehk)	to agree (with)
être en train de ehtr ahN traN duh	to be busy (doing something)
être sur le point de ehtr sewr luh pwaN duh	to be about to
faire attention à fehr ah-tahN-syohN ah	to pay attention to
faire beau fehr bo	to be nice weather
faire chaud fehr cho	to be hot weather
faire des achats fehr day zah-shah	to go shopping
faire du vent fehr dew vahN	to be windy
faire frais fehr freh	to be cool weather
faire froid fehr frwah	to be cold weather
faire la connaissance de fehr lah koh-neh-sahNs duh	to become acquainted with
faire mauvais feh mo-veh	to be bad weather
faire un voyage fehr uhN vwah-yahzh	to take a trip

continues

faire une partie de fehr ewn pahr-tee duh	to play a game of
faire une promenade fehr ewn prohm-nahd	to take a walk, a ride
n'en pouvoir plus nahN poo-vwahr plew	to be exhausted
valoir la peine (de) (+ infinitive) vah-lwahr lah pehn (duh)	to be worthwhile (to)
valoir mieux (+ infinitive) vah-lwahr myuh	to be better (to)
venir de vuh-neer duh	to have just (in the present and imperfect tenses)
vouloir dire voo-lwahr deer	to mean
y être ee ehtr	to understand, see

The following are some examples of these idioms.

Je n'en peux plus.
zhuh nahN puh plew

I'm exhausted.

Qu'est-ce que ça veut dire?
kehs kuh sah vuh deer

What does that mean?

Tu y es?
tew ee eh

Do you understand?

Ils viennent d'arriver.
eel vyehn dah-ree-vay

They just arrived.

Other Idioms

Some idiomatic expressions begin with prepositions and refer to time, travel, location, and direction. Others enable you to express your feelings and opinions about things. The following list provides common idioms that should come in quite handy.

à (with time expressions) ah	goodbye, until
à demain ah duh-maN	see you tomorrow
à jamais ah zhah-meh	forever
à l'heure ah luhr	on time
à partir de ah pahr-teer duh	from … on … beginning (with) …
à peu près ah puh preh	nearly, about, approximately
à propos de, au sujet de ah proh-po duh, o soo-zheh duh	about, concerning
à quoi bon (+ infinitive) … ? ah kwah bohN	what's the use of … ?
à tout à l'heure ah too tah luhr	see you in a little while
au contraire o kohN-trehr	on the contrary
au revoir o ruh-vwahr	goodbye, see you again
bien entendu, bien sûr byaN nahN-tahN-dew, byaN sewr	of course
bon marché bohN mahr-shay	cheap
C'est entendu. seh tahN-tahN-dew	It's agreed. All right.

continues

c'est-à-dire seh tah deer	that is to say
Cela m'est égal. suh-lah meh tay-gahl	It makes no difference to me. That's all the same to me.
Cela ne fait rien. suh-lah nuh feh ryaN	That doesn't matter. It makes no difference.
d'abord dah-bohr	first, at first
D'accord. dah-kohr	Agreed. Okay.
de bonne heure duh boh nuhr	early
de la part de duh lah pahr duh	on behalf of, from
de nouveau duh noo-vo	again
de quelle couleur … ? duh kehl koo-luhr	what color … ?
De rien. duh ryaN	You're welcome.
Il n'y a pas de quoi. eel nyah pah duh kwah	Don't mention it.
en (+ means of transport) ahN	by
en effet ahN neh-feh	(yes) indeed, as a matter of fact
en même temps ahN mehm tahN	at the same time
en retard ahN ruh-tahr	late (not on time)
en tout cas ahN too kah	in any case, at any rate
encore une fois ahN-kohr ewn fwah	again
et ainsi de suite ay aN-see duh sweet	and so forth
grâce à grahs ah	thanks to

il y a (+ time) eel yah	ago
meilleur marché meh-yuhr mahr-shay	cheaper
n'importe naN-pohrt	no matter, never mind
par conséquent pahr kohN-say-kahN	therefore, consequently
par exemple pahr ehgz-ahNpl	for example
par hasard pahr ah-zahr	by chance
peu à peu puh ah puh	little by little, gradually
peut-être puh tehtr	perhaps, maybe
quant à kahN tah	as for
quel kehl	what, what a
sans doute sahN doot	without a doubt
s'il vous plaît seel voo pleh	please
tant mieux tahN myuh	so much the better
tant pis tahN pee	so much the worse, too bad
tous (les) deux too (lay) duh	both
tout à (d'un) coup too tah (duhN) koo	suddenly
tout à fait too tah feh	entirely, quite
tout de même tood mehm	all the same
tout de suite toot sweet	immediately
tout le monde too luh mohNd	everybody

continues

The following are some examples of these idioms.

Au revoir. À demain.
o ruh-vwahr ah duh-maN

Goodbye. See you tomorrow.

Il voyage en avion.
eel vwah-yahzh ahN nah-vyohN

He's traveling by plane.

Je le répéterai encore une fois.
zhuh luh ray-pay-tray ahN-kohr ewn fwah

I'll repeat it again.

Je te rappelle tout de suite.
zhuh tuh rah-pehl toot-sweet

I'll call you back immediately.

Slang

The following idiomatic phrases might be considered mild slang.

Big deal!	*Et alors!* ay ah-lohr
Cut it out!	*Ça suffit!* sah sew-fee
Get out of here!	*Va-t'en!* vah-tahN
Get over it!	*Passe à autre chose!* pahs ah otr shoz
Good riddance!	*Bon débarras!* bohN day-bah-rah
I'm really fed up!	*J'en ai ras le bol!* zahN nay rah luh bohl

I've had it up to here!	*J'en ai marre!* zhahN nay mahr
It goes without saying.	*Il va sans dire.* eel vah sahN deer
It's a pleasure.	*Je vous en prie.* zhuh voo zahN pree
It's not worth it.	*Ça ne vaut pas la peine.* sah nuh vo pah lah pehn
Keep your shirt on!	*Ne t'énerve pas!* nuh tay-nehrv pah
Knock it off!	*Arrête!* ah-reht
Leave me alone!	*Laisse-moi tranquille!* lehs-mwah trahN-keel
Make up your mind!	*Décide-toi!* day-seed-twah
Mind your own business!	*Mêle-toi de tes affaires!* mehl-twah duh tay zah-fehr
Never mind!	*Ne t'en fais pas!* nuh tahN feh pah
No kidding?	*Sans blague?* sahN blahg
No way!	*Pas question!* pah kehs-tyohN
Of course!	*Bien sûr!* byaN sewr
Oh no!	*Mais non!* meh nohN
Shame on you! (You have no shame!)	*Tu n'as pas honte!* tew nah pah zohNt
Thank heavens!	*Grâce au ciel!* grahs o syehl
That bugs me!	*Ça me dérange!* sah muh day-rahNzh
That infuriates me!	*Ça me fait rager!* sah me feh rah-zhay
That's going too far!	*Cela dépasse les bornes!* suh-lah day-pahs lay bohrn
That's the last straw!	*Ça, c'est la goutte d'eau!* sah seh lah goot do

continues

There's no doubt.	*Il n'y a pas le moindre doute.* eel nyah pah luh mwaNdr doot
Wow!	*Oh là là!* oh lah lah
You bet!	*C'est clair!* seh klehr
You can say that again!	*C'est le cas de le dire!* seh luh kah duh luh deer
You must be kidding!	*Tu me fais marcher!* tew muh feh mahr-shay
You're driving me nuts!	*Tu me rends fou (folle)!* tew muh rahN foo (fohl)
You're too much!	*C'est trop fort!* seh tro fohr

Chapter 4

Quick Grammar

To be able to express yourself in French, you don't have to memorize and mentally translate pages of rules or walk around with a dictionary under your arm. On the contrary, it's best to learn language patterns naturally—the way a native speaker does. To do this, however, you need to know a few basic grammar rules. This chapter will get you started.

Nouns

Nouns name people, places, things, and ideas. They can be replaced by pronouns (*he, she, it,* and *they*). In French, all nouns have a gender (masculine or feminine) and a number (singular or plural). Articles (*a, an,* and *the*) serve as noun identifiers and usually help indicate gender and number.

Gender

Use the following articles and demonstrative adjectives to express *the, a (an),* and *this* or *that* before masculine and feminine nouns.

	Masculine Singular	Feminine Singular
the	*le* luh	*la* lah
a (an)	*un* uhN	*une* ewn
this, that	*ce* suh	*cette* seht

Le and *la* become *l'* before a vowel. *Ce* becomes *cet* before a vowel.

> *L'ami de Robert et l'amie de Claire arrivent.*
> lah-mee duh roh-behr ay lah-mee duh klehr ah-reev

Robert's friend and Claire's friend arrive.

Some nouns can be either masculine or feminine depending on whether the speaker is referring to a male or a female. Just change the article without changing the spelling of the noun.

le touriste	*la touriste*
un enfant	*une enfant*

Forming Plurals

If a French noun refers to more than one person, place, thing, or idea, it can be made plural—just like in English. It's not enough to simply change the noun—the identifying article must also be plural.

	Masculine	Feminine
the	*les* lay	*les* lay
some	*des* day	*des* day
these, those	*ces* say	*ces* say

Because the same plural noun markers are used for masculine and feminine nouns, they don't enable you to determine gender. They only indicate that the speaker is referring to more than one noun. This means you must learn each noun with its singular article.

To form most plurals, add an unpronounced *s* to the singular form.

Singular	Plural
le garçon luh gahr-sohN	*les garçons* lay gahr-sohN
un garçon uhN gahr-sohN	*des garçons* day gahr-sohN
ce garçon suh gahr-sohN	*ces garçons* say gahr-sohN
la fille lah fee-y	*les filles* lay fee-y
une fille ewn fee-y	*des filles* day fee-y
cette fille seht fee-y	*ces filles* say fee-y

continues

Singular	Plural
l'enfant lahN-fahN	*les enfants* lay zahN-fahN
un enfant uhN nahN-fahN	*des enfants* day zahN-fahN
cet enfant seht ahN-fahN	*ces enfants* say zahN-fahN

French uses *s*, *x*, and *z* to make plurals. If a noun ends in one of these letters, no change is required.

le prix luh pree	*les prix* lay pree

le fils luh fees	*les fils* lay fees

Subject Pronouns

Pronouns take the place of nouns. The following are the French subject pronouns.

Singular	Plural
je (I) zhuh	*nous* (we) noo
tu (you) (familiar) tew	*vous* (you) (polite) voo
il (he) eel	*ils* (they) eel
elle (she) ehl	*elles* (they) ehl

Quels sont tes pronoms?
kehl sohN tay proh-nohN

What are your pronouns?

Je vais en France.
zhuh veh zahN frahNs

I'm going to France.

Le français est facile.
luh frahN-seh eh fah-seel

French is easy.

Il est facile.
eel eh fah-seel

It's easy.

La femme parle anglais.
lah fahm pahrl ahN-gleh

The woman speaks English.

Elle parle anglais.
ehl pahrl ahN-gleh

She speaks English.

Verbs

Verbs are words that indicate actions or states of being. Subjects can be nouns or pronouns.

When speaking about a mixed-gender group, always use the masculine plural regardless of the number of males in the group.

Tu is used when speaking to a relative, close friend, child, or pet. In all other instances, use the polite form *vous*. *Vous* is also used when "you" is plural—whether speaking informally or formally.

Verbs are often shown as infinitives—the basic "to" form of the verb: to live, to laugh, to love. The infinitive is the verb form before it's conjugated. Conjugation is changing the ending of a verb to agree with the subject and show tense (past, present, etc.).

Verbs can be regular (most verbs with the same ending follow the same rules) or irregular (there are no rules, so you must memorize them). Regular verbs belong to one of three large families: those with infinitives ending in -*er*, -*ir*, or -*re*.

The Present Tense

The present tense, which you'll be using most frequently, has three main functions.

* Expresses what generally happens all the time:

  Je regarde la télévision tous les jours.
  zhuh ruh-gahrd lah tay-lay-vee-zyohN too lay zhoor

  I watch television every day.

* Expresses events taking place at present:

  Mes amis vont au cinéma.
  may zah-mee vohN to see-nay-mah

  My friends are going to the movies.

* Implies actions or events that will occur in the immediate future:

  Je te parle plus tard.
  zhuh tuh pahrl plew tahr

  I'll speak to you later.

The Present Tense of Regular Verbs

Subject	-er Verbs (parler)	-ir Verbs (finir)	-re Verbs (répondre)
je	parle pahrl	finis fee-nee	réponds ray-pohN
tu	parles pahrl	finis fee-nee	réponds ray-pohN
il, elle	parle pahrl	finit fee-nee	répond ray-pohN
nous	parlons pahr-lohN	finissons fee-nee-sohN	répondons ray-pohN-dohN
vous	parlez pahr-lay	finissez fee-nee-say	répondez ray-pohN-day
ils, elles	parlent pahrl	finissent fee-nees	répondent ray-pohNd

The following four high-frequency verbs are irregular in the present tense.

	aller (to go)	avoir (to have)	être (to be)	faire (to make, to do)
je (j')	vais veh	ai ay	suis swee	fais feh
tu	vas vah	as ah	es eh	fais feh
il, elle	va vah	a ah	est eh	fait feh
nous	allons ah-lohN	avons ah-vohN	sommes sohm	faisons feh-zohN
vous	allez ah-lay	avez ah-vay	êtes eht	faites feht
ils, elles	vont vohN	ont ohN	sont sohN	font fohN

The Compound Past Tense (*Le passé composé*)

Use the compound past tense in the following ways.

- To express an action or event that began or was completed at a specific time in the past, even if the time isn't mentioned:

  Le film a commencé a huit heures.
  luh feelm ah koh-mahN-say ah wee tuhr

  The film began at 8:00.

  Il est arrivé en retard.
  eel eh tah-ree-vay ahN ruh-tard

  He arrived late.

- To express an action or event that was repeated a stated number of times:

  Je suis allé en France deux fois.
  zhuh swee zah-lay ahN frahNs duh fwah

  I went to France two times.

The compound past tense has two parts:

- **Helping verb:** This expresses that an action *has* taken place. In most instances, the French use *avoir* as the helping verb. Verbs of motion (those showing action that indicates a change) use *être* as their helping verb. Helping verbs are conjugated in their present tense forms. (See page 37.)

- **Past participle:** This expresses an action that *happened*. It's added after the conjugated helping verb. To form the past participle of regular verbs, drop the infinitive ending (-*er*, -*ir*, -*re*) and add the following endings.

-*er* Verbs	-*ir* Verbs	-*re* Verbs
danser (to dance)	*finir* (to finish)	*perdre* (to lose)
*dans**é***	*fin**i***	*perd**u***

Ils ont dansé.
eel zohN dahN-say

They danced.

J'ai fini mon travail.
zhay fee-nee mohN trah-vah-y

I finished my work.

Elle a perdu sa clé.
ehl ah pehr-dew sah klay

She lost her key.

To form the compound past tense of irregular verbs, add an irregular past participle to the conjugated helping verb. The following are the most common.

Past participles ending in -*u*

avoir	*eu*	had
boire	*bu*	drank
lire	*lu*	read
recevoir	*reçu*	received
voir	*vu*	seen, saw

Past participles ending in *-is*

mettre	*mis*	put, put on
prendre	*pris*	took

Past participles ending in *-it*

dire	*dit*	said, told
écrire	*écrit*	written, wrote

Irregular past participles

être	*été*	been, was
faire	*fait*	made, done, did

The following verbs use *être* as their helping verb.

Infinitive	Past Participle	Meaning
aller	*allé* ah-lay	went
arriver	*arrivé* ah-ree-vay	arrived
descendre	*descendu* day-sahN-dew	went down
devenir	*devenu* duh-vnew	became
entrer	*entré* ahN-tray	entered
monter	*monté* mohN-tay	went up
mourir	*mort* mohr	died
naître	*né* nay	was born
partir	*parti* pahr-tee	tleft
passer	*passé* pah-say	passed (by)
rentrer	*rentré* rahN-tray	returned

rester	*resté* rehs-tay	remained
retourner	*retourné* ruh-toor-nay	returned
revenir	*revenu* ruh-vnew	returned
sortir	*sorti* sohr-tee	went out
tomber	*tombé* tohN-bay	fell
venir	*venu* vnew	came

The compound past tense is formed by conjugating the helping verb and adding the past participle.

When *avoir* is the helping verb, the past participle generally remains constant.

> *J'ai fait un voyage.*
> zhay feh tuhN vwah-yahzh

I took a trip.

> *Elles ont fait un voyage.*
> ehl zohN feh tuhN vwah-yahzh

They took a trip.

However, when *être* is the helping verb, the past participle must agree in number and gender with the subject. If the subject is feminine, add an *e*. If the subject is plural, add an *s*.

Masculine Subject	Feminine Subject	Meaning
je suis tombé	*je suis tombée*	I fell (have fallen)
tu es venu	*tu es venue*	you came (have come)
il est mort	*elle est morte*	he/she (has) died

continues

Masculine Subject	Feminine Subject	Meaning
nous sommes allés	*nous sommes allées*	we went (have gone)
vous êtes revenu(s)	*vous êtes revenue(s)*	you (have) returned
ils sont sorti	*elles sont sorties*	they (have) left

The Imperfect

The imperfect expresses continuous or repeated actions, events, situations, or states in the past. It's used in the following ways.

- To describe what was happening or used to happen again and again in the past:

  Les enfants jouaient.
  lay zahN-fahN zhoo-eh

  The children were playing.

  J'allais au musée le samedi.
  zhah-leh o mew-zay luh sahm-dee

  I used to go to the museum on Saturday.

- To express an ongoing past action:

  Elle travaillait le soir.
  ehl trah-vah-yeh luh swahr

  She worked at night.

- To describe people, things, or time in the past:

  Sa mère était très belle.
  sah mehr ay-teh treh behl

  His mother was very beautiful.

La rue était déserte.
lah rew ay-teh day-zehrt

The street was deserted.

Il était cinq heures de l'après-midi.
eel ay-teh saN kuhr duh lah-preh-mee-dee

It was 5:00 in the afternoon.

- To express a state of mind in the past
  with such verbs as *croire* (to believe),
  penser (to think), *pouvoir* (to be able to),
  vouloir (to want), and *savoir* (to know):

  Elle voulait aller à l'université.
  ehl voo-leh ah-lay ah lew-nee-vehr-see-tay

  She wanted to go to the university.

- To describe a situation that was going on in
  the past when another action occurred:

  Je lisais quand le téléphone a sonné.
  zhuh lee-zeh kahN luh tay-lay-fohn ah soh-nay

  I was reading when the telephone rang.

To form the imperfect of a regular verb, drop the
-ons ending from the present tense *nous* form of
the verb and add the following endings.

je	*-ais*	*nous*	*-ions*
tu	*-ais*	*vous*	*-iez*
il, elle	*-ait*	*ils, elles*	*-aient*

The following are some examples.

	-er Verbs (nous dansons)	-ir Verbs (nous finissons)	-re Verbs (nous attendons)
je	dansais dahN-seh	finissais fee-nee-seh	attendais ah-tahN-deh
tu	dansais dahN-seh	finissais fee-nee-seh	attendais ah-tahN-deh
il, elle	dansait dahN-seh	finissait fee-nee-seh	attendait ah-tahN-deh
nous	dansions dahN-syohN	finissions fee-nee-syohN	attendions ah-tahN-dyohN
vous	dansiez dahN-syay	finissiez fee-nee-syay	attendiez ah-tahN-dyay
ils, elles	dansaient dahN-seh	finissaient fee-nee-seh	attendaient ah-tahN-deh

The only irregular verb in the imperfect is *être*.

j'étais	nous étions
tu étais	vous étiez
il était	ils étaient

The Future

The future can be expressed in the following ways.

* Using the present to imply the future:

  Elles arrivent ce soir.
  ehl zah-reev suh swahr

  They're arriving tonight.

* Using *aller* (to go) + the infinitive of a verb:

   Ils vont arriver ce soir.
   eel vohN tah-ree-vay suh swahr

   They're going to arrive tonight.

* Using the future tense:

   Ils arriveront ce soir.
   eel zah-reev-rohN suh swahr

   They'll arrive tonight.

Form the future tense by adding the future endings
to the infinitive of regular verbs. For verbs ending
in *-re*, drop the final *e* from the infinitive.

je	*-ai*	*nous*	*-ons*
tu	*-as*	*vous*	*-ez*
il, elle	*-a*	*ils, elles*	*-ont*

   Ils voyageront demain.
   eel vwah-yahzh-rohN duh-maN

   They'll travel tomorrow.

   Je réfléchirai.
   zhuh ray-flay-shee-ray

   I'll think about it.

   Nous vendrons notre voiture.
   noo vahN-drohN nohtr vwah-tewr

   We'll sell our car.

Adjectives

Adjectives are used to describe nouns. All French adjectives must agree in number and gender with the nouns they modify. You can form the feminine of most adjectives by adding an *e* to the masculine form. In most cases, the feminine adjective will have a different sound than the masculine adjective, where the final ending consonant is pronounced.

L'homme est blond.
lohm eh blohN

The man is blond.

La femme est blonde.
lah fahm eh blohNd

The woman is blonde.

Le livre est amusant.
luh leevr eh tah-mew-zahN

The book is amusing.

La pièce est amusante.
lah pyehs eh tah-mew-zahNt

The play is amusing.

But:

Ce sac est joli.
suh sahk eh zhoh-lee

This bag is pretty.

Cette robe est jolie.
seht rohb eh zhoh-lee

This dress is pretty.

When an adjective ends in an -*e* in its masculine form, it's not necessary to make any changes at all to get the feminine form. Both are spelled and pronounced exactly the same.

Cet acteur est célèbre.
seh tahk-tuhr eh say-lehbr

This actor is famous.

Cette actrice est célèbre.
seh tahk-trees eh say-lehbr

This actress is famous.

When a masculine adjective ends in -*x*, the feminine is formed by changing *x* to *se*, which gives the feminine ending a *z* sound.

Il est heureux.
eel eh tuh-ruh

He's happy.

Elle est heureuse.
ehl eh tuh-ruhz

She's happy.

When a masculine adjective ends in -*f*, the feminine is formed by changing *f* to *ve*.

Ce garçon est actif.
suh gahr-sohN eh tahk-teef

That boy is active.

Cette fille est active.
seht fee-y eh tahk-teev

That girl is active.

When a masculine adjective ends in *-er*,
the feminine is formed by changing *er* to *ère*,
with no change in pronunciation.

> *Ce bracelet est cher.*
> suh brahs-leh eh shehr

This bracelet is expensive.

> *Cette bague est chère.*
> seht bahg eh shehr

This ring is expensive.

Some masculine adjectives double the last consonant
and add *e* to form the feminine. Note the pronounced
consonant for the feminine form.

> *Ce gâteau est bon.*
> suh gah-to eh bohN

This cake is good.

> *Cette tarte est bonne.*
> seht tahrt eh bohn

This tart is good.

Some adjectives you'll encounter will have
irregular forms.

> *Le garçon est beau.*
> luh gahr-sohN eh bo

The boy is handsome.

> *La fille est belle.*
> lah fee-y eh behl

The girl is beautiful.

Le camion est blanc.
luh kah-myohN eh blahN

The truck is white.

La voiture est blanche.
lah vwah-tewr eh blahNsh

The car is white.

Le melon est doux.
luh muh-lohN eh doo

The melon is sweet.

La pêche est douce.
lah pehsh eh doos

The peach is sweet.

Ce quartier est vieux.
suh kahr-tyay eh vyuh

This neighborhood is old.

Cette ville est vieille.
seht veel eh vyay

This city is old.

Most adjectives become plural by adding an unpronounced *s* to the singular: *timides* (tee-meed), *charmant(e)s* (shahr-mahN[t]), *joli(e)s* (zhoh-lee), *fatigué(e)s* (fah-tee-gay).

If an adjective ends in *-s* or *-x*, it's not necessary to add the *s*: *exquis* (ehks-kee), *heureux* (uh-ruh).

Most masculine singular adjectives ending in *-al* change the *al* to *aux* in the plural: *spéciaux* (spay-syo).

If an adjective ends in *-eau*, add *x* to form the plural.

Le garçon est beau.
luh gahr-sohN eh bo

The boy is handsome.

Les garçons sont beaux.
lay gahr-sohN sohN bo

The boys are handsome.

Most French adjectives are placed after the nouns
they modify—the opposite of English.

un homme intéressant
uhN nohm aN-tay-ray-sahN

an interesting man

Adjectives showing the following qualities generally
go before the nouns they modify.

BEAUTY: *beau* (bo), *joli* (zhoh-lee)

AGE: *jeune* (zhuhn), *nouveau* (noo-vo), *vieux* (vyuh)

GOODNESS (or lack of it): *bon* (bohN), *gentil*
(zhahN-teey), *mauvais* (mo-veh), *villain* (vee-laN)

SIZE: *grand* (grahN), *petit* (puh-tee), *court* (koor),
long (lohN), *gros* (gro), *large* (lahrzh)

un jeune garçon
uhN zhuhn gahr-sohN

a young boy

une large avenue
ewn lahrzh ahv-new

a wide avenue

Adverbs

Adverbs are words that describe verbs, adjectives, or other adverbs. In English, most adverbs end in *-ly*: He dances slowly. However, in French, they end in *-ment*: *Il danse lentement.*

Add *ment* to the masculine singular forms of adjectives that end in a vowel.

The following are some examples.

Adjective	Adverb	Meaning
passionné pah-syoh-nay	*passionnément* pah-syoh-nay-mahN	enthusiastically
rapide rah-peed	*rapidement* rah-peed-mahN	rapidly, quickly
vrai vreh	*vraiment* vreh-mahN	truly, really

If the masculine form of the adjective ends in a consonant, first change it to the feminine form and then add *ment*. The following chart shows how to form adverbs from feminine adjectives.

Adjective	Adverb	Meaning
active ahk-teev	*activement* ahk-teev-mahN	actively
complète kohN-pleht	*complètement* kohN-pleht-mahN	completely
continuelle kohN-tee-new-ehl	*continuellement* kohN-tee-new-ehl-mahN	continually
douce doos	*doucement* doos-mahN	sweetly, gently
fière fyehr	*fièrement* fyehr-mahN	proudly
franche frahNsh	*franchement* frahNsh-mahN	frankly

continues

Adjective	Adverb	Meaning
lente lahNt	*lentement* lahNt-mahN	slowly
sérieuse say-ryuhz	*sérieusement* say-ryuhz-mahN	seriously
seule suhl	*seulement* suhl-mahN	only

Some adverbs are formed by changing a silent *e* from the adjective to *é* before the *-ment* ending.

Adjective	Adverb	Meaning
énorme ay-nohrm	*énormément* ay-nohr-may-mahN	enormously

Adjectives ending in *-ant* and *-ent* have adverbs ending in *-amment* and *-emment*, respectively.

Adjective	Adverb	Meaning
constant kohN-stahN	*constamment* kohN-stah-mahN	constantly
récent ray-sahN	*récemment* ray-sah-mahN	recently

If you can't think of the adverb or if one doesn't exist, use the phrases *d'une façon* (dewn fah-sohN) or *d'une manière* (dewn mah-nyehr), which express "in a way," "in a manner, or "in a fashion."

> *Il parle d'une façon (d'une manière) intelligente.*
> eel pahrl dewn fah-sohN (dewn mah-nyehr) aN-teh-lee-zhahNt

> He speaks intelligently (in an intelligent way).

Some adverbs aren't formed from adjectives at all and therefore don't end in *-ment*. For example: *bientôt* (byaN-to, soon), *beaucoup* (bo-koo, much), *maintenant* (maNt-nahN, now).

Position of Adverbs

Adverbs are generally placed after the verbs they modify. Sometimes, however, the position of the adverb is variable and is usually where we'd logically put an English adverb.

> *D'habitude, il joue bien au football.*
> dah-bee-tewd eel zhoo byaN o foot-bol

Generally, he plays football well.

> *Il joue très bien au football.*
> eel zhoo treh byaN o foot-bol

He plays football very well.

Prepositions

Prepositions show the relationship between a noun and another word in a sentence.

The prepositions *à* and *de* contract with *le* and *les*.

> *à + le = au*   *de + le = du*

> *Je vais au cinéma.*
> zhuh veh zo see-nay-mah

I go to the movies.

> *Je parle du film.*
> zhuh pahrl dew feelm

I talk about the film.

à + les = aux   *de + les = des*

Elle va aux magasins.
ehl vah o mah-gah-zaN

She goes to the stores.

Elle achète des souvenirs.
ehl ah-sheht day soov-neer

She buys souvenirs.

Chapter 5

The Basics

This chapter provides the essential words and expressions you'll need for everyday situations: using numbers, telling time, expressing dates (days of week, months, seasons), asking about and expressing the weather, using formal and informal greetings and salutations, being polite, and getting information.

Numbers

Cardinal Numbers

0	*zéro* zay-ro
1	*un* uhN
2	*deux* duh
3	*trois* trwah
4	*quatre* kahtr
5	*cinq* saNk
6	*six* sees
7	*sept* seht
8	*huit* weet
9	*neuf* nuhf
10	*dix* dees
11	*onze* ohNz
12	*douze* dooz
13	*treize* trehz
14	*quatorze* kah-tohrz
15	*quinze* kaNz
16	*seize* sehz

17	*dix-sept* dee-seht
18	*dix-huit* dee-zweet
19	*dix-neuf* dee-znuhf
20	*vingt* vaN
21	*vingt et un* vaN tay uhN
22	*vingt-deux* vaN-duh
30	*trente* trahNt
40	*quarante* kah-rahNt
50	*cinquante* saN-kahNt
60	*soixante* swah-sahNt
70	*soixante-dix* swah-sahNt-dees
71	*soixante et onze* swah-sahN tay ohNz
72	*soixante-douze* swah-sahNt-dooz
73	*soixante-treize* swah-sahNt-trehz
74	*soixante-quatorze* swah-sahNt-kah-tohrz
75	*soixante-quinze* swah-sahNt-kaNz
76	*soixante-seize* swah-sahNt-sehz
77	*soixante-dix-sept* swah-sahNt-dee-seht
78	*soixante-dix-huit* swah-sahNt-dee-zweet
79	*soixante-dix-neuf* swah-sahNt-dee-znuf

continues

80	*quatre-vingts* kahtr-vaN
81	*quatre-vingt-un* kahtr-vaN-uhN
82	*quatre-vingt-deux* kahtr-vaN-duh
90	*quatre-vingt-dix* kahtr-vaN-dees
91	*quatre-vingt-onze* kahtr-vaN-onze
92	*quatre-vingt-douze* kahtr-vaN-dooz
100	*cent* sahN
101	*cent un* sahN uhN
200	*deux cents* duh sahN
201	*deux cent un* duh sahN uhN
1,000	*mille* meel
2,000	*deux mille* duh meel
1,000,000	*un million* uhN mee-lyohN
2,000,000	*deux millions* duh mee-lyohN
1,000,000,000	*un milliard* uhN mee-lyahr
2,000,000,000	*deux milliards* duh mee-lyahr

In numerals, where Americans use commas, French speakers use periods. Where Americans use decimal points, French speakers use commas.

English	$1,009.95
French	$1.009,95

The conjunction *et* (and) is used for the numbers
21, 31, 41, 51, 61, and 71. Use a hyphen in all other
compound numbers through 99.

> 21   *vingt et un*
>
> 32   *trente-deux*
>
> 81   *quatre-vingt-un*

Un becomes *une* before a feminine noun.

> 1 boy   *un garçon*
>
> 1 girl   *une fille*

To form 71–79, use 60 + 11, 12, 13, etc.

> 71   *soixante et onze*
>
> 74   *soixante-quatorze*

To form 91–99, use 80 (4 × 20) + 11, 12, 13, etc.

> 91   *quatre-vingt-onze*
>
> 94   *quatre-vingt-quatorze*

Un (one) isn't used before *cent* and *mille*.

> 100 men   *cent hommes*
>
> 1,000 women   *mille femmes*

Million adds an -*s* for the plural and must be
followed by *de* before a noun.

> 1,000,000 people   *un million de gens*
>
> 2,000,000 people   *deux millions de gens*

Ordinal Numbers

first	*premier (première)* pruh-myay (pruh-myehr)
second	*deuxième (second[e])* duh-zyehm (suh-gohN[d])
third	*troisième* trwah-zyehm
fourth	*quatrième* kah-tree-yehm
fifth	*cinquième* saN-kyehm
sixth	*sixième* see-zyehm
seventh	*septième* seh-tyehm
eighth	*huitième* wee-tyehm
ninth	*neuvième* nuh-vyehm
tenth	*dixième* dee-zyehm

Ordinal numbers agree in gender and number with the noun they modify. *Premier* and *second* are the only ordinal numbers that have a feminine form.

> *son premier (second) roman*
 sohN pruh-myay (suh-gohN) roh-mahN
>
> his (her) first (second) novel

> *sa première (seconde) chanson*
 sah pruh-myehr (suh-gohnd) shahN-sohN
>
> his (her) first (second) song

Except for *premier* and *second*, add *-ième* to a cardinal number to form the ordinal number. Drop any silent *e* before *-ième*.

> fourth   *quatrième*

A -*u* is added to *cinquième* and a *v* replaces the *f* in *neuvième*.

Second(e) is generally used in a series that doesn't go beyond two.

their second house

leur seconde maison
luhr suh-gohNd meh-zohN

Elision doesn't occur (the definite article *le* or *la* doesn't drop its vowel) with *huitième* and *onzième*.

le huitième mois
luh wee-tyehm mwah

the eighth month

la onzième année
lah ohN-zyehm ah-nay

the eleventh year

Telling Time

What time is it?	*Quelle heure est-il?* kehl uhr eh-teel
At what time?	*À quelle heure?* ah kehl uhr
It's 1:00.	*Il est une heure.* eel eh tew nuhr
It's 2:05.	*Il est deux heures cinq.* eel eh duh zuhr saNk
It's 3:10.	*Il est trois heures dix.* eel eh trwah zuhr dees
It's 4:15.	*Il est quatre heures et quart.* eel eh kahtr uhr ay kahr
It's 5:20.	*Il est cinq heures vingt.* eel eh saN kuhr vaN

continues

It's 6:25.	*Il est six heures vingt-cinq.* eel eh see zuhr vaN-saNk
It's 7:30.	*Il est sept heures et demie.* eel eh seh tuhr ay duh-mee
It's 7:35.	*Il est huit heures moins vingt-cinq.* eel eh wee tuhr mwaN vaN-saNk
It's 8:40.	*Il est neuf heures moins vingt.* eel eh nuh vuhr mwaN vaN
It's 9:45.	*Il est dix heures moins le quart.* eel eh dee zuhr mwaN luh kahr
It's 10:50.	*Il est onze heures moins dix.* eel eh ohN zuhr mwaN dees
It's 11:55.	*Il est midi moins cinq.* eel eh mee-dee mwaN saNk
It's noon.	*Il est midi.* eel eh mee-dee
It's midnight.	*Il est minuit.* eel eh mee-nwee

You might hear the time expressed as follows.

> *Il est sept heures quarante.*
> eel eh seh tuhr kah-rahNt
>
> It's 7:40.

Use the following for half past noon or midnight.

> *Il est midi et demi.*
> eel eh mee-dee ay duh-mee
>
> *Il est minuit et demi.*
> eel eh mee-nwee ay duh-mee

Use *demie* to express half past with all other hours.

The following expressions are helpful when referring to the time in general.

a second	*une seconde* ewn suh-gohNd
a minute	*une minute* ewn mee-newt
an hour	*une heure* ew nuhr
in the morning (a.m.)	*du matin* dew mah-taN
in the afternoon (p.m.)	*de l'après-midi* duh lah-preh-mee-dee
in the evening (p.m.)	*du soir* dew swahr
at exactly midnight	*à minuit précis* ah mee-nwee pray-see
at exactly 1:00	*à une heure précise* ew nuhr uhr pray-seez
at exactly 2:00	*à deux heures précises* ah duh zuhr pray-seez
at about 2:00	*vers deux heures* vehr duh zuhr
at 3:00	*à trois heures* ah trwah zuhr
a quarter of an hour	*un quart d'heure* uhN kahr duhr
a half hour	*une demi-heure* ewn duh-mee-uhr
in an hour	*dans une heure* dahN zew nuhr
until 2:00	*jusqu'à deux heures* zhew-skah duh zuhr
before 3:00	*avant trois heures* ah-vahN trwah zuhr
after 3:00	*après trois heures* ah-preh trwah zuhr
since (from) what time	*depuis quelle heure* duh-pwee keh luhr
since (from) 6:00	*depuis six heures* duh-pwee see zuhr
an hour ago	*il y a une heure* eel yah ew nuhr

continues

per hour	*par heure*
	pah ruhr
early	*tôt (de bonne heure)*
	to (duh boh nuhr)
late (in the day)	*tard*
	tahr
late (in arriving)	*en retard*
	ahN ruh-tahr
on time	*à l'heure*
	ah luhr

Days of the Week

Monday	*lundi*
	luhN-dee
Tuesday	*mardi*
	mahr-dee
Wednesday	*mercredi*
	mehr-kruh-dee
Thursday	*jeudi*
	zhuh-dee
Friday	*vendredi*
	vahN-druh-dee
Saturday	*samedi*
	sahm-dee
Sunday	*dimanche*
	dee-mahNsh

In French, the days of the week are only capitalized at the beginning of a sentence. Elsewhere, unlike in English, they're lowercased.

> *Samedi est mon jour favori.*
> sahm-dee eh mohN zhoor fah-voh-ree

Saturday is my favorite day.

> *Je ne travaille pas samedi prochain.*
> zhuh nuh trah-vah-y pah sahm-dee proh-shehn

I'm not working next Saturday.

Use the definite article *le* to express that something does (or doesn't) occur "on" a specific day.

> *Je ne travaille pas le samedi.*
> zhuh nuh trah-vah-y pah luh sahm-dee

> I'm not working on Saturday.
> (I don't work on Saturdays.)

Months

January	*janvier*	zhahN-vyay
February	*février*	fay-vryay
March	*mars*	mahrs
April	*avril*	ah-vreel
May	*mai*	meh
June	*juin*	zhwaN
July	*juillet*	zhwee-eh
August	*août*	oo(t)
September	*septembre*	sehp-tahNbr
October	*octobre*	ohk-tohbr
November	*novembre*	noh-vahNbr
December	*décembre*	day-sahNbr

Like days of the week, unless used at the beginning of a sentence, months should be lowercased. To say that something is expected to happen in a certain month, use the preposition *en*.

> *Juillet est mon mois favori.*
> zhwee-yeh eh mohN mwah fah-voh-ree

July is my favorite month.

> *Je vais en France en avril.*
> zhuh veh zahN frahNs ahN nah-vreel

I'm going to France in April.

Dates

Use the following when you have to refer to a date.

> What day is it (today)?
>
> *Quel jour est-ce (aujourd'hui)?*
> kehl zhoor ehs (o-zhoor-dwee)

> What's the date? (What's today's date?)
>
> *Quelle est la date? (Quelle est d'aujourd'hui?)*
> kehl eh lah daht (kehl eh do-zhoor-dwee)

Use the following to express the date.

> day of the week + *le*
> + (cardinal) number + month + year

> Today is Monday, October 11, 2021.
>
> *C'est aujourd'hui lundi le onze octobre deux mille vingt et un.*
> seh to-zhoor-dwee luhN-dee luh ohNz ohk-tohbr duh meel vaN-tay-uhN

Use *premier* to express the first of each month.
Use cardinal numbers for all other days.

> *le premier juin*
> luh pruh-myay zwaN
>
> June 1st
>
> *le deux juin*
> luh duh zwaN
>
> June 2nd

Use the definite article *le* to express "on" with dates.

> *J'arrive le trois mai.*
> zhah-reev luh trwah meh
>
> I'm arriving on May 3rd.

Just as in English, years are usually expressed in
hundreds. When the word for "thousand" is written
in dates only, *mil* is often used instead of *mille* for
dates before 2000.

> 1989
>
> *mille neuf cent quatre-vingt-neuf*
> meel nuf sahN kahtr-vaN-nuhf
>
> nineteen hundred eighty-nine
>
> *dix neuf cent quatre-vingt-neuf*
> deez-nuhf sahN kahtr-vaN-nuhf

In French, the date is written by reversing
the month/day sequence used in English.

le 5 janvier 2013	5/1/13
January 5, 2013	1/5/13

Seasons

autumn (fall)	*l'automne* lo-tohn
spring	*le printemps* luh praN-tahN
summer	*l'été* lay-tay
winter	*l'hiver* lee-vehr

The French use the preposition *en* to express "in" for seasons (except for spring, when *au* is used).

> *Elle va à Paris en hiver (en été, en automne, au printemps).*

She's going to Paris in the winter (in the summer, in the fall, in the spring).

Weather

What's the weather?	*Quel temps fait-il?* kehl tahN feh-teel
It's beautiful.	*Il fait beau.* eel feh bo
It's hot.	*Il fait chaud.* eel feh sho
It's sunny.	*Il fait du soleil.* eel feh dew soh-leh-y
It's nasty (bad).	*Il fait mauvais.* eel feh mo-veh
It's cold.	*Il fait froid.* eel feh frwah
It's cool.	*Il fait frais.* eel feh freh
It's windy.	*Il fait du vent.* eel feh dew vahN
It's lightning.	*Il fait des éclairs.* eel feh day zay-klehr

It's thundering.	*Il fait du tonnerre.* eel feh dew toh-nehr
It's foggy.	*Il y a du brouillard.* eel yah dew broo-yahr
It's humid.	*Il fait humide.* eel feh tew-meed
It's cloudy.	*Il y a des nuages.* eel yah day new-ahzh
It's overcast.	*Le ciel est couvert.* luh syehl eh koo-vehr
It's raining.	*Il pleut.* eel pluh
It's pouring.	*Il pleut à verse.* eel pluh ah vehrs
It's snowing.	*Il neige.* eel nehzh
There are gusts of wind.	*Il y a des rafales.* eel yah day rah-fahl
There's hail.	*Il y a de la grêle.* eel yah duh lah grehl
There are sudden showers.	*Il y a des giboulées.* eel yah day zhee-boo-lay

Greetings & Salutations

Formal Salutations

Hello. (Good Morning.)	*Bonjour.* bohN-zhoor
Good evening.	*Bonsoir.* bohN-swahr
Mr., sir	*Monsieur* muh-syuh
Mrs., madam, woman	*Madame* mah-dahm
Miss, young woman	*Mademoiselle* mahd-mwah-zehl
My name is … .	*Je m'appelle … .* zhuh mah-pehl

continues

What's your name?	*Comment vous appelez-vous?* koh-mahN voo zah-play-voo
How are you?	*Comment allez-vous?* koh-mahN tah-lay-voo
Very well, thank you.	*Très bien, merci.* treh byaN mehr-see
Not bad.	*Pas mal.* pah mahl
Nice to meet you.	*Enchanté.* (male speaker) / *Enchantée.* (female speaker) ahN-shahN-tay
The pleasure is mine.	*Moi de même.* mwah duh mehm
Goodbye.	*Au revoir.* o ruh-vwahr
See you soon.	*À bientôt.* ah byaN-to

Informal Salutations

Hi.	*Salut.* sah-lew
My name is … .	*Je m'appelle … .* zhuh mah-pehl
What's your name?	*Comment t'appelles-tu?* koh-mahN tah-pehl-tew
How are you?	*Comment vas-tu?* koh-mahN vah-tew
How's it going?	*Ça va?* sah vah
What's new?	*Quoi de neuf?* kwah duh nuhf
Nothing much.	*Rien de spécial.* ryaN duh spay-syahl
See you later.	*À tout à l'heure.* ah too tah luhr

Being Polite

Please.	*S'il vous plaît.* seel voo pleh
Thank you (very much).	*Merci (beaucoup).* mehr-see (bo-koo)
You're welcome.	*De rien. (Pas de quoi.)* duh ryaN (pah-duh-kwah)
Don't mention it. (Not at all.) (You're welcome.)	*Je vous en prie.* zhuh voo zahN pree
Excuse me.	*Pardon. (Excusez-moi.)* pahr-dohN (ehks-kew-zay mwah)
I'm sorry.	*Je suis désolé(e).* zhuh swee day-zoh-lay
I'm sorry to bother you.	*Je suis désolé(e) de vous déranger.* zhuh swee day-zoh-lay duh voo day-rahN-zhay
If you don't mind.	*Si ça ne vous fait rien.* see sah nuh voo feh ryaN
Bless you! (after sneezing)	*À vos souhaits!* ah vo sweh

Asking "Yes" or "No" Questions

There are four ways to ask questions that require a "Yes" or "No" answer.

Intonation

By far the easiest way to show that you're asking a question is to simply change your intonation by raising your voice at the end of a sentence.

Vous parlez anglais?
voo pahr-lay ahN-gleh

Do you speak English?

N'est-ce pas?

You can also add *n'est-ce pas* (nehs pah), meaning
"isn't that so," at the end of a sentence.

Vous parlez anglais, n'est-ce pas?
voo pahr-lay ahN-gleh nehs-pah

You speak English, don't you (isn't that so)?

Est-ce que

You can put *est-ce que* (ehs-kuh) at the beginning
of a sentence. It's not translated, but *est-ce que*
indicates that a question follows.

Est-ce que vous parlez anglais?
ehs-kuh voo pahr-lay ahN-gleh

Do you speak English?

Inversion

Inversion, which is used far more frequently in
writing than in conversation, means reversing
the word order of the subject pronoun and the
conjugated verb form. The following are the rules
for inversion.

- Avoid inverting with *je*. (Although certain
  cases exist where this is acceptable.)

- You can only invert subject pronouns with
  conjugated verbs. Don't invert with nouns.

Vous parlez anglais.
voo pahr-lay ahN-gleh

You speak English.

Parlez-vous anglais?
pahr-lay-voo ahN-gleh

Do you speak English?

* With *il* and *elle*, a -*t*- must be added to avoid two vowels together.

Il parle anglais.
eel pahrl ahN-gleh

He speaks English.

Parle-t-il anglais?
pahrl-teel ahN-gleh

Does he speak English?

Asking for Information

Use the following phrases to get information.

à quelle heure ah keh luhr	at what time
à qui ah kee	to whom
à quoi ah kwah	to what
avec qui ah-vehk kee	with whom
avec quoi ah-vehk kwah	with what
de qui duh kee	of, about, from whom

continues

de quoi duh kwah	of, about, from what
combien (de) kohN-byaN (duh)	how much, many
comment koh-mahN	how
où oo	where
d'où doo	from where
pourquoi poor-kwah	why
quand kahN	when
qu'est-ce que kehs-kuh	what
que kuh	what
qui kee	who, whom
quoi kwah	what

Use *que* at the beginning of a sentence and *quoi* at the end of a sentence to ask "what."

> *Que fais-tu?*
> kuh feh-tew

> *Tu fais quoi?*
> tew feh kwah

> What are you doing?

Use the following to obtain information.

- Use intonation:

> *Vous parlez (Tu parles) avec qui?*
> voo pahr-lay (tew pahrl) ah-vehk kee

> With whom are you speaking?

- Use *est-ce que*:

  Avec qui est-ce que vous parlez (tu parles)?
  ah-vehk kee ehs-kuh voo pahr-lay (tew pahrl)

  With whom are you speaking?

- Use inversion:

  Avec qui parlez-vous (parles-tu)?
  ah-vehk kee pahr-lay voo (pahrl-tew)

  With whom are you speaking?

Beginners will find the following phrases useful when needing to give and get information.

Do you speak English?	*Parlez-vous anglais?* pahr-lay-voo ahN-gleh
Does anyone speak English?	*Il y a quelqu'un qui parle anglais?* eel yah kehl-kuhN kee pahrl ahN-gleh
Do you understand me?	*Vous me comprenez?* voo muh kohN-pruh-nay
I speak (a little) French.	*Je parle (un peu) français.* zhuh pahrl (uhN puh) frahN-seh
I don't speak French.	*Je ne parle pas français.* zhuh nuh pahrl pah frahN-seh
I (don't) understand.	*Je (ne) comprends (pas).* zhuh (nuh) kohN-prahN (pah)
I'm don't understand anything.	*Je n'y comprends rien.* zhuh nee kohN-prahN ryaN
I need an interpreter.	*Il me faut un interprète.* eel muh fo tuhN naN-tehr-preht
I didn't hear you.	*Je ne vous ai pas entendu.* zhuh nuh voo zay pah zahN-tahN-dew
Please speak more slowly.	*Parlez plus lentement s'il vous plaît.* pahr-lay plew lahNt-mahN seel voo pleh

continues

Please repeat.	*Répétez s'il vous plaît.* ray-pay-tay seel voo pleh
What did you say?	*Qu'est-ce que vous avez dit?* kehs-kuh voo zah-vay dee
What does that mean?	*Que veut dire ça?* kuh vuh deer sah
How do you say … in French?	*Comment dit-on …* *en français?* koh-mahN dee tohN … ahN frahN-seh
Can you write that down?	*Pouvez-vous écrire cela?* poo-vay voo ay-kreer suh-lah
How do you spell that?	*Comment épelez-vous cela?* koh-mahN tay-play-voo suh-lah
Can you help me?	*Pouvez-vous m'aider?* poo-vay-voo may-day
I need help.	*J'ai besoin d'aide.* zhay buh-zwaN dehd
I have a problem.	*J'ai un problème.* zhay uhN proh-blehm
What's this?	*Qu'est-ce que c'est?* kehs-kuh seh
Where's the lost and found?	*Où se trouve le bureau* *d'objets trouvés?* oo suh troov luh bew-ro dohb-zheh troo-vay

Personal Profile

You might find yourself in different situations
where you need to convey personal information in
French: your name, nationality, occupation, family
relationships, hobbies, and pastimes. You might
even need some of this information to participate
on social media sites. This chapter will help you do
all that and more.

Names

My name is … .	*Je m'appelle* … . zhuh mah-pehl
What's your name? (polite)	*Comment vous appelez-vous?* kohN-mah voo zah-play voo
What's your name? (familiar)	*Comment t'appelles-tu?* kohN-mah tah-pehl tew
What's your last (birth) (married last) name?	*Quel est ton nom de famille* *(naissance) (mariage)?* kehl eh tohN nohN duh fah-mee-y (neh-sahNs) (mah-ree-ahzh)

Countries of Origin & Nationalities

Where are you from? (polite)	*D'où êtes-vous?* doo eht-voo
Where are you from? (familiar)	*D'où es-tu?* doo eh-tew
I'm (We're) … .	*Je suis (Nous sommes)* … . zhuh swee (noo sohm)

Use the following to express "from" a place.

de before	feminine countries	*de France*
	feminine continents	*d'Europe*
	feminine provinces	*de Bretagne*
	feminine islands	*de Corse*
	masculine countries beginning with a vowel	*d'Israël*
	cities	*de Pittsburgh*
du before	masculine countries	*du Canada*
de l' before	modified continents	*de l'Amérique du Sud*
des before	plural countries	*des États-Unis*

I'm from France (the United States, Spain, Mexico, Haiti).

Je suis de France (des États-Unis, d'Espagne, du Mexique, d'Haïti).

Use the following tables to express a person's nationality. The first spelling and pronunciation are masculine. The letter(s) and pronunciation in parentheses are feminine. Nationalities that end in -*e* stay the same regardless of gender. Add a silent -*s* (except for nationalities that end in -*s*) for all plurals. Use the following examples to guide you.

He's English.

Il est anglais.
eel eh tahN-gleh

She's English.

Elle est anglaise.
ehl eh tahN-glehz

We [m.] are English.

Nous sommes anglais.
noo sohm zahN-gleh

We [f.] are English.

Nous sommes anglaises.
noo sohm zahN-glehz

Feminine Countries & Nationalities

Algeria	*Algérie* ahl-zhay-ree	*algérien(ne)(s)* ahl-zhay-ryaN (-ryehn)
Austria	*Autriche* o-treesh	*autrichien(ne)(s)* o-tree-shyaN (-shyehn)
Belgium	*Belgique* behl-zheek	*belge(s)* behlzh
China	*Chine* sheen	*chinois(e)(s)* shee-nwah(z)
Egypt	*Égypte* ay-zheept	*égyptien(ne)(s)* ay-zheep-syaN (-syehn)
England	*Angleterre* ahN-gluh-tehr	*anglais(e)(s)* ahn-gleh(z)
France	*France* frahNs	*français(e)(s)* frahN-seh(z)
Germany	*Allemagne* ahl-mah-nyuh	*allemand(e)(s)* ahl-mahN(d)

Greece	*Grèce* grehs	*grec(s) (grecque[s])* grehk
India	*Inde* aNd	*indien(ne)(s)* aN-dyaN (-dyehn)
Italy	*Italie* ee-tah-lee	*italien(ne)(s)* ee-tah-lyaN (-yehn)
Norway	*Norvège* nohr-vehzh	*norvégien(ne)(s)* nohr-vay-zyaN (zyehn)
Russia	*Russie* rew-see	*russe(s)* rews
Scotland	*Écosse* ay-kohs	*écossais(e)(s)* ay-koh-seh(z)
Spain	*Espagne* ehs-pah-nyuh	*espagnol(e)(s)* ehs-pah-nyohl
Sweden	*Suède* swehd	*suédois(e)(s)* sway-dwah(z)
Switzerland	*Suisse* swees	*suisse(s)* swees
Tunisia	*Tunisie* tew-nee-zee	*tunisien(ne)(s)* tew-nee-zyaN (-zyehn)

Masculine Countries & Nationalities

Canada	*Canada* kah-nah-dah	*canadien(ne)(s)* kah-nah-dyaN (-dyehn)
Cambodia	*Cambodge* kahN-bohdzh	*cambodgien(ne)(s)* kahm-bohd-zhyaN (-zhyehn)
Denmark	*Danemark* dahn-mahrk	*danois(e)(s)* dah-nwah(z)
Haiti	*Haïti* ah-ee-tee	*haïtien(ne)(s)* ah-ee-syaN (-syehn)
Israel	*Israël* eez-rah-ehl	*israélien(ne)(s)* eez-rah-ay-lyaN (-lyehn)
Japan	*Japon* zhah-pohN	*japonais(e)(s)* zhah-poh-neh(z)
Lebanon	*Liban* lee-bahN	*libanais(e)(s)* lee-bah-neh(z)
Morocco	*Maroc* mah-rohk	*marocain(e)(s)* mah-roh-kaN (-kehn)

continues

Mexico	*Mexique* mehks-eek	*mexicain(e)(s)* mehks-ee-kaN (-kehn)
Netherlands	*Pays-Bas* pay-ee bah	*néerlandais(e)(s)* nay-ehr-lahN-deh(z)
Portugal	*Portugal* pohr-tew-gahl	*portugais(e)(s)* pohr-tew-geh(z)
Senegal	*Sénégal* say-nay-gahl	*sénégalais(e)(s)* say-nay-gah-leh(z)
United States	*États-Unis* ay-tah-zew-nee	*américain(e)(s)* ah-may-ree-kaN (-kehn)

Continents

The continents are feminine except for Antarctica.

Africa	*l'Afrique* lah-freek
Antarctica	*l'Antarctique* (m.) lahN-tahrk-teek
Asia	*l'Asie* lah-zee
Australia	*l'Australie* lo-strah-lee
Europe	*l'Europe* luh-rohp
North America	*l'Amérique du Nord* lah-may-reek dew nohr
South America	*l'Amérique du Sud* lah-may-reek dew sewd

Occupations

Many professions that end in *e* can refer to males
or females. Just change the pronoun according to
the gender. Feminine forms are listed in parentheses
in the table starting on the next page.

> *Il est comptable.*
> eel eh kohN-tahbl
>
> He's an accountant.

> *Elle est comptable.*
> ehl eh kohN-tahbl
>
> She's an accountant.

> *Il est acteur.*
> eel eh tahk-tuhr
>
> He's an actor.

> *Elle est actrice.*
> ehl eh tahk-trees
>
> She's an actress.

> *Il est boulanger.*
> eel eh boo-lahN-zhay
>
> He's a baker.

> *Elle est boulangère.*
> ehl eh boo-lahN-zhehr
>
> She's a baker.

To refer to a woman in a profession that always uses the masculine word form, indicated by "(m.)," simply add the word *femme* (fahm) before the job title.

> *Elle est femme pilote.*
> ehl eh fahm pee-loht

She's a female pilot.

What's your profession?	*Quel est votre métier?* kehl eh vohtr may-tyay
I'm a (an) …	*Je suis …* zhuh swee
accountant.	*comptable.* kohn-tahbl
actor (actress).	*acteur (actrice).* ahk-tuhr (ahk-trees)
architect.	*architecte.* ahr-shee-tehkt
artist.	*artiste.* ahr-teest
baker.	*boulanger (-gère).* boo-lahN-zhay (-zhehr)
banker.	*banquier (-quière).* bahN-kyay (-kyehr)
businessman (businesswoman).	*homme (femme) d'affaires.* ohm (fahm) dah-fehr
butcher.	*boucher (-chère).* boo-shay (-shehr)
cashier.	*caissier (-ière).* kehs-yay (-yehr)
computer scientist.	*informaticien(ne).* aN-fohr-mah-tee-syaN (-syehn)
dentist.	*dentiste.* dahN-teest
doctor.	*docteur(e). / (médecin).* dohk-tuhr / mayd-saN
electrician.	*électricien (-ciene).* ay-lehk-tree-syaN (-syehn)

engineer.	*ingénieur(e).* ahN-zhay-nyuhr
firefighter.	*pompier (-pière).* pohN-pyay (-pyehr)
government employee.	*fonctionnaire.* fohNk-syoh-nehr
hairdresser.	*coiffeur (-feuse).* kwah-fuhr (-fuhz)
jeweler.	*bijoutier (-tière).* bee-zhoo-tyay (-tyehr)
lawyer.	*avocat(e).* ah-voh-kah(t)
mail carrier.	*facteur (-trice).* fahk-tuhr (-trees)
manager.	*gérant(e).* zhay-rahN(t)
mechanic.	*mécanicien (-cienne).* may-kah-nee-syaN (-syehn)
musician.	*musicien (-cienne).* mew-zee-syaN (-syehn)
nurse.	*infirmier (-mière).* ahN-feer-myay (-myehr)
optician.	*opticien (-cienne).* ohp-tee-syaN (-syehn)
photographer.	*photographe.* foh-toh-grahf
pilot.	*pilote.* pee-loht
plumber.	*plombier (-bière).* plohN-byay (-byehr)
police officer.	*agent(e) de police.* ah-zhahN(t) duh poh-lees
postal worker.	*postier (-ière).* pohs-tyay (-tyehr)
programmer.	*programmeur (-meuse).* proh-grah-muhr (-muhz)
retired.	*à la retraite.* ah lah ruh-treht
salesperson.	*vendeur (-deuse).* vahN-duhr (-duhz)

continues

secretary.	*secrétaire.* seh-kray-tehr
server.	*serveur (-veuse).* sehr-vuhr (-vuhz)
student.	*étudiant(e).* ay-tewd-yahN(t)
surgeon.	*chirurgien (-giene).* shee-rewr-zhyahN (-zyehn)
teacher.	*professeur.* proh-feh-suhr
veterinarian.	*vétérinaire.* vay-tay-ree-nehr

The indefinite article *un* (*une*) isn't used with
a profession unless it's qualified by an adjective.

Elle est artiste.
ehl eh tahr-teest

She's an artist.

Elle est une artiste célèbre.
ehl eh tewn ahr-teest say-lehbr

She's a famous artist.

I'm in the …	*Je suis dans …* zhuh swee dahN
army.	*l'armée.* lahr-may
navy.	*la marine.* lah mah-reen
air force.	*l'armée de l'air.* lahr-may duh lehr
marines.	*les marines.* lay mah-reen

I work part-time.

Je travaille à temps partiel.
zhuh trah-vah-y ah tahN pahr-syehl

I'm semi-retired.

Je suis semi-retraité(e).
zhuh swee suh-mee-ruh-treh-tay

Physical Descriptions

Feminine forms as well as plural endings and forms are in parentheses.

What do you look like? (polite)	*Comment êtes-vous?* koh-mahN eht-voo
What do you look like? (familiar)	*Comment es-tu?* koh-mahN eh-tew
I'm … years old.	*J'ai … ans.* zhay … ahN
I'm short (tall).	*Je suis petit(e) (grand[e]).* zhuh swee puh-tee(t) (grahN[d])
I weigh (about) … pounds (kilograms).	*Je pèse (environ) … livres (kilogrammes).* zhuh pehz (ahN-vee-rohN) … leevr (kee-loh-grahm)
I'm … feet … inches (meters) tall.	*Je mesure … pieds … pouces (mètres).* zhuh muh-zoor … pyay … poos (mehtr)
I have … hair.	*J'ai les cheveux … .* zhay lay shuh-vuh
long	*longs* lohN
short	*courts* koor
curly	*bouclés* boo-klay
straight	*lisses* lees
dark	*foncés* fohN-say

continues

light	*clairs* klehr
black	*noirs* nwahr
blond	*blonds* blohN
brown	*bruns* bruhN
gray	*gris* gree
red	*roux* roo
I'm bald.	*Je suis chauve.* zhuh swee shov
I have … eyes.	*J'ai les yeux …* zhay lay zyuh
blue	*bleus.* bluh
brown	*marron.* mah-rohN
dark	*foncés.* fohN-say
light	*clairs.* klehr
gray	*gris.* gree
green	*verts.* vehr
hazel	*noisette.* nwah-zeht
I have a moustache (beard).	*J'ai une moustache (barbe).* zhay ewn moo-stahsh (bahrb)
I have a tattoo (tattoos).	*J'ai un tatouage (des tatouages).* zhay ewn tah-twahzh (day tah-twahzh)
I have a piercing (piercings.)	*J'ai un piercing (des piercings).* zhay uhN peer-seeng (day peer-seeng)

I'm ...	*Je suis ...* zhuh swee
single.	*célibataire.* say-lee-bah-tehr
married.	*marié(e).* mah-ree-yay
separated.	*séparé(e).* sapah-ray
divorced.	*divorcé(e).* dee-vohr-say
widowed.	*veuf (veuve).* vuhf (vuhv)
I have one child (two children).	*J'ai un enfant (deux enfants).* zhay uhN nahN-fahN (duh zahN-fahN)
I don't have any children.	*Je n'ai pas d'enfants.* zhuh nay pah dahN-fahN
I have a dog (cat).	*J'ai un chien (chat).* zhay uhN shyahN (shah)

Personality Traits

I'm ...	*Je suis ...* zhuh swee
ambitious.	*ambitieux (-tieuse).* ahN-bee-syuh (-syuhz)
athletic.	*sportif (-tive).* spohr-teef (-teev)
courteous.	*courtois(e).* koor-twah(z)
daring.	*audacieux (-ieuse).* o-dah-syuh(z)
efficient.	*efficace.* ay-fee-kahs
extroverted.	*extraverti(e).* ehks-trah-vehr-tee
friendly.	*aimable.* eh-mahbl

continues

funny.	*drôle.* drol
generous.	*généreux (-euse).* zhay-nah-ruh(z)
happy.	*heureux (-euse).* uh-ruh(z)
honest.	*honnête.* oh-neht
impulsive.	*impulsif (-sive).* aN-pool-seef (-seev)
introverted.	*introverti(e).* aN-troh-vehr-tee
kind.	*gentil(le).* zhahN-tee(-y)
open.	*ouvert(e).* oo-vehr(t)
optimistic.	*optimiste.* ohp-tee-meest
pessimistic.	*pessimiste.* peh-see-meest
proud.	*fier (-ère).* fyehr
punctual.	*ponctuel(le).* pohNk-tew-ehl
realistic.	*réaliste.* ray-ah-leest
reasonable.	*raisonnable.* reh-zoh-nahbl
responsible.	*responsable.* rehs-pohN-sahbl
shy.	*timide.* tee-meed
sincere.	*sincère.* saN-sehr
sociable.	*sociable.* soh-syahbl
talkative.	*bavard(e).* bah-vahr(d)

Hobbies & Pastimes

I like to ...	*J'aime ...* zhehm
bake.	*faire de la pâtisserie.* fehr duh lah pah-tees-ree
cook.	*cuisiner.* kwee-zee-nay
dance.	*danser.* dahN-say
draw.	*dessiner.* day-see-nay
go running.	*courir.* koo-reer
go shopping.	*faire du shopping* *(magasiner).* fehr dew shoh-peeng (mah-gah-zee-nay)
go to concerts.	*aller aux concerts.* ah-lay o kohn-sehr
go to museums.	*aller aux musées.* ah-lay o mew-zay
go to the ballet.	*aller au ballet.* ah-lay o bah-leh
go to the beach.	*aller à la plage.* ah-lay ah lah plahzh
go to the movies.	*aller au cinéma.* ah-lay o see-nay-mah
go to the opera.	*aller à l'opéra.* ah-lay ah loh-pay-rah
go to the theater.	*aller au théâtre.* ah-lay o tay-ahtr
knit.	*tricoter.* tree-koh-tay
listen to music.	*écouter de la musique.* ay-koo-tay duh lah mew-zeek
paint.	*peindre.* paNdr

continues

play cards.	*jouer aux cartes.* hoo-ay o kahrt
play checkers.	*jouer aux dames.* zhoo-ay o dahm
play chess.	*jouer aux échecs.* zhoo-ay o zay-shehk
play golf.	*jouer au golf.* zhoo-ay o gohlf
play sports.	*faire du sport.* faire dew spohr
play tennis.	*jouer au tennis.* zhoo-ay o tay-nees
read.	*lire.* leer
sew.	*coudre.* koodr
ski.	*faire du ski.* fehr dew skee
swim.	*nager.* nah-zhay
take pictures.	*prendre des photos.* prahNdr day foh-to
travel.	*voyager.* vwah-yah-zhay
write.	*écrire.* ay-kreer

Feelings

I'm …	*Je suis …* zhuh swee
angry.	*fâché(e).* fah-shay
anxious.	*anxieux (-ieuse).* aNks-yuh (-yuhz)
delighted.	*ravi(e).* rah-vee
depressed.	*déprimé(e).* day-pree-may

displeased.	*mécontent(e).* may-kohN-tahN(t)
flattered.	*flatté(e).* flah-tay
furious.	*furieux (-rieuse).* few-ryuh (-ryuhz)
grateful.	*reconnaissant(e).* ruh-koh-neh-sahN(t)
happy.	*heureux (-euse).* uh-ruh(z)
irritated.	*irrité(e).* ee-ree-tay
jealous.	*jaloux (-se).* zhah-loo(z)
surprised.	*surpris(e).* sewr-pree(z)
unhappy.	*malheureux (-reuse).* mahl-uh-ruh(z)
worried.	*inquiet (-iète).* aN-kee-yeh(t)

Note that the following feelings use the verb *avoir*.

J'ai peur.
zhay puhr

I'm afraid.

J'ai honte.
zhay ohNt

I'm ashamed.

Family Members

I'd like to introduce …	*Je voudrais présenter …* zhuh voo-dreh pray-zahN-tay
my aunt.	*ma tante.* mah tahNt
my boyfriend.	*mon petit ami.* mohN puh-tee-tah-mee
my brother.	*mon frère.* mohN frehr
my child.	*mon enfant.* mohN nahN-fahN
my cousin.	*ma cousine.* (female) / *mon cousin.* (male) mah koo-zeen / mohN koo-zahN
my daughter.	*ma fille.* mah fee-y
my daughter-in-law.	*ma belle-fille.* mah behl fee-y
my father.	*mon père.* mohN pehr
my father-in-law.	*mon beau-père.* mohN bo-pehr
my girlfriend.	*ma petite amie.* mah puh-tee-tah-mee
my granddaughter.	*ma petite-fille.* mah puh-teet-fee-y
my grandfather.	*mon grand-père.* mohN grahN-pehr
my grandmother.	*ma grand-mère.* mah grahN-mehr
my grandson.	*mon petit-fils.* mohN puh-tee-fees
my half brother.	mon demi-frère mohN duh-mee-frehr
my half sister.	ma demi-sœur mah duh-mee-suhr
my husband.	*mon mari.* mohN mah-ree

my mother.	*ma mère.* mah mehr
my mother-in-law.	*ma belle-mère.* mah behl-mehr
my nephew.	*mon neveu.* mohN nuh-vuh
my niece.	*ma nièce.* mah nyehs
my parent.	*mon parent.* mohN pah-rahN
my partner.	*ma compagne.* (female) / *mon compagnon.* (male) mah kohN-pah-nyuh / mohN kohN-pah-nyohN
my sister.	*ma sœur.* mah suhr
my son.	*mon fils.* mohN fees
my son-in-law.	*mon beau-fils.* mohN bo-fees
my spouse.	*mon époux(-se).* mohN nay-poo(z)
my stepbrother (my brother-in-law).	*mon beau-frère.* mohN bo-frehr
my stepdaughter.	*ma belle-fille.* mah behl-fee-y
my stepfather.	*mon beau-père.* mohN bo-pehr
my stepmother.	*ma belle-mère.* mah behl-mehr
my stepparent.	*mon beau-parent.* mohN bo-pah-rahN
my stepsister (my sister-in-law).	*ma belle-sœur.* mah behl-suhr
my stepson.	*mon beau-fils.* mohN bo-fees
my uncle.	*mon oncle.* mohN nohNkl
my wife.	*ma femme.* mah fahm

continues

Use *mes* to express "my" when referring to plurals.

mes enfants
may zahN-fahN

my children

mes parents
may pah-rahN

my parents

mes grands-parents
may grahN-pah-rahN

my grandparents

mes beaux-parents
may bo-pah-rahN

my in-laws

Possessive Adjectives

Unlike in English, French possessive adjectives agree with the nouns they modify, not the subject.

Elle présente son frère.
ehl pray-zahNt sohN frehr

She introduces her brother.

Il adore ses enfants.
eel ah-dohr say zahN-fahN

He adores his children.

Use the masculine singular possessive adjective before all singular nouns beginning with a vowel.

Il parle à son amie.
eel pahrl ah sohN nah-mee

He speaks to his female friend (girlfriend).

Singular		Plural	Meaning
MASCULINE	FEMININE		
mon mohN	*ma* mah	*mes* may	my
ton tohN	*ta* tah	*tes* tay	your
son sohN	*sa* sah	*ses* say	his, her
notre nohtr	*notre* nohtr	*nos* no	our
votre vohtr	*votre* vohtr	*vos* vo	your
leur luhr	*leur* luhr	*leurs* luhr	their

Social Media

May I email (text) you?	*Puis-je t'envoyer un email (texto)?* pweezh tahN-vwah-yay uhN ee-mehl (tehks-to)
What's your email address?	*Quelle est ton adresse email?* kehl eh tohN nah-drehs ee-mehl
What's your cell phone number?	*Quel est ton numéro de portable (mobile) (cellulaire)?* kehl eh tohN new-may-ro duh pohr-tahbl (moh-beel) (seh-lew-lehr)
I'm on Facebook (Twitter) (Instagram).	*Je suis sur Facebook (Twitter) (Instagram).* zhuh swee sewr Facebook (Twitter) (Instagram)

continues

Follow me on Facebook (Twitter) (Instagram).	*Suis-moi sur Facebook (Twitter) (Instagram).* swee-mwah sewr Facebook (Twitter) (Instagram)
(I) I'll follow you.	*Je te suis.* zhuh tuh swee
I'd like to friend you on Facebook.	*Je voudrais t'envoyer une invitation à être ami(e)s sur Facebook.* zhuh voo-dreh tahN-vwah-yay ewn aN-vee-tah-syohN ah ehtr ah-mee sewr Facebook
Go to my Facebook (Instagram) (Twitter) page.	*Va sur ma page Facebook (Instagram) (Twitter).* vah sew mah pahzh Facebook (Instagram) (Twitter)
Look at my profile page.	*Regarde ma page de profil.* ruh-gahrd mah pahzh duh proh-feel
I post (share) my pictures on Facebook (Instagram).	*Je poste (partage) mes photos sur Facebook (Instagram).* zhuh pohst (pahr-tahzh) may foh-to sewr Facebook (Instagram)
Can I post your picture on Facebook (Instagram)?	*Puis-je poster ta photo sur Facebook (Instagram)?* pweezh pohs-tay tah foh-to sewr Facebook (Instagram)
I read your post (yours).	*J'ai lu ton message (le tien).* zhay lew tohN meh-sahzh (luh tyaN)
Did you read my post (mine)?	*As-tu lu mon message (le mien)?* ah-tew lew mohN meh-sahzh (luh myaN)
Send me a message.	*Envoie-moi un message.* ahN-vwah-mwah uhN meh-sahzh
Do you want to chat?	*Veux-tu bavarder?* vuh-tew bah-vahr-day
FaceTime (Skype) me.	*Appelle-moi sur FaceTime (Skype).* ah-pehl mwah sewr FaceTime (Skype)

Chapter 7

Travel

If you're planning a trip to France or to another French-speaking country or area, the following lists will enable you to get information for air, boat, bus, subway, train, taxi, and car travel.

Air Travel

At Security

Here's my boarding pass and my passport.	*Voici ma carte d'embarquement et mon passeport.* vwah-see mah kahrt dahN-bahrk-mahN ay mohN pahs-pohr
Do I have to remove my shoes (my coat, my belt)?	*Dois-je enlever mes chaussures (mon manteau) (ma ceinture)?* dwahzh ahN-lvay may sho-sewr (mohN mahN-to) (mah saN-tewr)
Do I have to open my suitcase (my backpack)?	*Dois-je ouvrir ma valise (mon sac à dos)?* dwahzh oo-vreer mah vah-leez (mohN sahk ah do)
I have a medical condition. Here's a note (prescription) from my doctor.	*J'ai un problème médical. Voici une note (ordonnance) de mon médecin.* zhay uhN proh-blehm may-dee-kahl vwah-see ewn noht (ohr-doh-nahNs) duh mohN mayd-saN

At the Travel Desk

When is there a flight to ... ?	*Quand y a-t-il un vol pour ...* kahN tee-ah-teel uhN vohl poor
Is it a direct flight?	*Est-ce un vol direct?* ehs uhN vohl dee-rehkt
Is there a stopover? Where?	*Y a-t-il une escale? Où?* ee-ah-teel ewn ehs-kahl oo
How long is the stopover?	*Combien de temps dure l'escale?* kohN-byaN duh tahN dewr lehs-kahl

I'd like ...	*Je voudrais ...* zhuh voo-dreh
a round-trip ticket.	*un aller-retour* uhN nah-lay-ruh-toor
a one-way ticket.	*un aller simple* uhN nah-lay saNpl
an economy class ticket.	*un billet en seconde classe* uhN bee-yeh ahN suh-gohNd klahs
a first-class ticket.	*un billet en première classe* uhN bee-yeh ahN pruh- myehr klahs
a business class ticket.	*un billet en classe affaires* uhN bee-yeh ahN klahs ah-fehr
a children's ticket.	*un billet au tarif enfant* un bee-yeh o tah-reef ahN-fahN
a student ticket.	*un billet au tarif étudiant* uhN bee-yeh o tah-reef ay-tew-dyahn
a senior ticket.	*un billet senior* uhN bee-yeh say-nyohr
I'd like a seat next to the window.	*Je voudrais une place à côté de la fenêtre.* zhuh voo-dreh ewn plahs ah ko-tay duh lah fuh-nehtr
I'd like a seat on the aisle.	*Je voudrais une place côté couloir.* zhuh voo-dreh ewn plahs ko-tay koo-lwahr
I need more leg room.	*J'ai besoin de plus d'espace pour les jambes.* zhay buh-zwaN duh plew dehs-pahs poor lay zhahNb
What's the fare?	*Quel est le tarif?* kehl eh luh tah-reef
Are taxes included?	*Les taxes sont comprises?* lay tahks sohN kohN-preez
What's the flight number?	*Quel est le numéro du vol?* kehl eh luh new-may-ro dew vohl

continues

When does the flight leave (arrive)?	*Le vol part (arrive) à quelle heure?* luh vohl pahr (ah-reev) ah kehl uhr
From what gate do we leave?	*De quelle porte partons-nous?* duh kehl pohrt pahr-tohN-noo
How long is the flight?	*Quelle est la durée du vol?* kehl eh lah dew-ray dew vohl
Are meals (snacks) (drinks) served?	*On sert des repas (en-cas) (boissons)?* ohN sehr day ruh-pas (ahN-kah) (bwah-sohN)
Is the flight going to leave (arrive) on time (late)?	*Le vol part (arrive) à l'heure (en retard)?* luh vohl pahr (ah-reev) ah luhr (ahN ruh-tahr)
I have only carry-on baggage.	*J'ai seulement des bagages à main.* zhay suhl-mahN day bah-gahzh ah maN
I'd like to check my bags.	*Je voudrais enregistrer mes bagages.* zhuh voo-dreh ahN-ruh-zhees-tray may bah-gahzh
Where do I check them?	*Où dois-je les enregistrer?* oo dwahzh lay zahN-ruh-zhees-tray
How much is it per bag?	*Quel est le tarif par valise?* kehl eh luh tah-reef pahr vah-leez

On the Plane

Where's ... ?	*Où est ... ?* oo eh
the bathroom	*les toilettes* lay twah-leht
the emergency exit	*la sortie de secours* lah sohr-tee duh suh-koor
the exit	*la sortie* lah sohr-tee

the life vest	*le gilet de sauvetage* luh zhee-leh duh sov-tahzh
the oxygen mask	*le masque à oxygène* luh mahsk ah ohks-ee-zhehn
the seat belt	*la ceinture de sécurité* lah saN-tewr duh say-kew-ree-tay

Arrival

Where's the baggage claim area?	*Où sont les bagages?* oo sohN lay bah-gahzh
Where can I get a baggage cart?	*Où puis-je trouver un chariot à bagages?* oo pweezh troo-vay uhN shah-ryo ah bah-gahzh
I'm looking for a porter.	*Je cherche un porteur.* zhuh shehrsh uhN pohr-tuhr
Where are the elevators?	*Où sont les ascenseurs?* oo sohN lay zah-sahN-suhr
Where are the escalators?	*Où sont les escaliers mécaniques?* oo sohN lay zehs-kah-lyay may-kah-neek
Where's the public transportation?	*Où est le transport public?* oo eh luh trahNs-pohr pewb-leek
Where's the car rental?	*Où est la location de voitures?* oo eh lah loh-kah-syohN duh vwah-tewrh
Where's customs?	*Où est la douane?* oo eh lah dwahn
Where can I get … ?	*Où puis-je prendre … ?* oo pweez prahNdr
a taxi	*un taxi* uhN tahks-ee
a train	*un train* uhN traN
a bus	*un bus* uhN bews

continues

the subway	*le métro* luh may-tro
a rideshare	*un covoiturage* uhN ko-vwah-tew-rahzh
Where can I change my money?	*Où puis-je changer mon argent?* oo pweezh shahN-zhay mohN nahr-zhahN
My suitcase is damaged.	*Ma valise est endommagée.* mah vah-leez eh tahN-doh-mah-zhay
I can't find my suitcase (my bags).	*Je ne peux pas trouver ma valise (mes bagages).* zhuh nuh puh pah troo-vay mah vah-leez (may bah-gahzh)
What should I do?	*Que dois-je faire?* kuh dwahzh fehr
Where should I go?	*Où dois-je aller?* oo dwahzh ah-lay

At Customs

I'm staying at the ... hotel.	*Je reste à l'hôtel ... .* zhuh rehst ah lo-tehl
I'm staying here ...	*Je reste ici ...* zhuh rehst ee-see
... days.	*... jours.* ... zhoor
a week.	*une semaine.* ewn suh-mehn
two weeks.	*deux semaines.* duh suh-mehn
a month.	*un mois.* uhN mwah
I'm on vacation.	*Je suis en vacances.* zhuh swee zahN vah-kahns
I'm visiting family.	*Je rends visite à ma famille.* zhuh rahN vee-zeet ah mah fah-mee-y
I'm on a business trip.	*Je suis en voyage d'affaires.* zhuh swee zahN vwah-yahzh dah-fehr

Here's ...	*Voici ...* vwah-see
my customs declaration form.	*mon formulaire de déclaration de douane.* mohN fohr-mew-lehr duh day-klah-rah-syohN duh dwahn
my passport.	*mon passeport.* mohN pahs-pohr
my driver's license.	*mon permis de conduire.* mohN pehr-mee duh kohN-dweer
I've nothing to declare.	*Je n'ai rien à déclarer.* zhuh nay ryaN ah day-klah-ray
May I close my suitcase (my suitcases)?	*Puis-je fermer ma valise (mes valises)?* pweezh fehr-may mah vah-leez (may vah-leez)

Boat Travel

At what time does the boat leave the port?	*Le bateau quitte le port à quelle heure?* luh bah-to keet luh pohr ah kehl uhr
What's the next port?	*Quel est le prochain port?* kehl eh luh proh-shaN pohr
How long does the crossing take?	*Combien de temps dure la traversée?* kohN-byaN duh tahN dewr lah trah-vehr-say
How long are we going to remain in port?	*Combien de temps allons-nous rester au port?* kohN-byaN duh tahN ah-lohN-noo rehs-tay o pohr
At what time do we have to be back on board?	*À quelle heure doit-on être de retour à bord?* ah kehl uhr dwah-tohN ehtr duh ruh-toor ah bohr

continues

What do you have for seasickness?	*Qu'est-ce que vous avez pour le mal de mer?* kehs-kuh voo zah-vay poor luh mahl duh mehr
At what time do we arrive in port?	*À quelle heure arrive-t-on au port?* ah kehl uhr ah-reev-tohN o pohr

Bus Travel

Many Parisian bus lines run through the center of the city, along the banks of the Seine, and through historic districts. The bus line number and the direction in which the bus is traveling are indicated on the front and on the sides of the bus. Electronic display signs at stops show the expected arrival time of the next bus. Service on some lines is limited in the evenings and on Sundays. The Noctilien is a night bus service that operates in and around Paris.

Bus tickets can be purchased at all metro stations, at most newsstands and tobacco stores, online at the Paris tourist office website (parisinfo.com), or on the bus itself. Remember to hold on to your ticket throughout your entire trip.

Where's the nearest bus stop?	*Où est l'arrêt de bus le plus proche?* oo eh lah-reh duh bews luh plew prohsh
How often do the buses run?	*Quelle est la fréquence des bus?* kehl eh lah fray-kahNs day bews
Does this bus goes to … ?	*Ce bus va à … ?* suh bews vah ah
How much is the fare?	*Quel est le tarif du trajet?* kehl eh luh tah-reef dew trah-zheh

Where can I buy a ticket?	*Où puis-je acheter un billet?* oo pweezh ahsh-tay uhN bee-yeh
Where do I have to get off?	*Où dois-je descendre?* oo dwahzh day-sahNdr
How many stops are there?	*Il y a combien d'arrêts?* eel yah kohN-byaN dah-reh
Do I have to transfer?	*Dois-je faire une correspondance?* dwahzh fehr ewn koh-rehs-pohN-danhs

Subway Travel

The subway is the least expensive, fastest, and easiest way to navigate Paris. There are 16 metro lines and about 300 stations, most of them easily identifiable by a large yellow M or a sign reading *Métro* or *Métropolitain*. Each subway line has a distinct color and number.

Transfers from one line to another are free as long as you don't exit through the turnstiles. Connections are indicated by *correspondance* (koh-rehs-pohN-dahNs) signs. Free maps are available throughout the city at metro stations, hotels, department stores, and tourist offices.

Where's the nearest subway station?	*Où est la station de métro la plus proche?* oo eh lah stah-syohN duh may-tro lah plew prohsh
Where can I buy a ticket?	*Où puis-je acheter un billet?* oo pweezh ahsh-tay uhN bee-yeh
How much is the fare?	*Quel est le tarif du trajet?* kehl eh luh tah-reef dew trah-zheh

continues

Where can I find a subway map?	*Où puis-je trouver un plan du métro?* oo pweezh troo-vay uhN plahN dew may-tro
Which line goes to … ?	*Quelle ligne va à … ?* kehl lee-nyuh vah ah
Do I have to change trains?	*Dois-je faire une correspondance?* dwahzh fehr ewn koh-rehs-pohN-dahNs
How many more stops are there?	*Il reste combien d'arrêts?* eel rehst kohN-byaN dah-reh
What's the next station?	*Quelle est la prochaine station?* kehl eh lah proh-shehehn stah-syohN
Where should I get off?	*Où dois-je descendre?* oo dwahzh day-sahNdr

Taxi & Rideshare Travel

Travel by taxi and rideshare is increasingly popular and is generally metered. Taxi rates vary according to the time of day and the location to which you're traveling. Tipping is optional but should be considered if the driver helped with your bags. When in doubt, if you're pleased with the service, consider rewarding your driver with a euro or two.

To express "to" for your destination:

- Use *à* before a proper name.

- Use *au* before a masculine singular noun beginning with a consonant.

- Use *à la* before a feminine singular noun beginning with a consonant.

- Use *à l'* before any singular noun beginning with a vowel.

- Use *aux* before all plural nouns.

Where's the nearest taxi stand?	*Où est le station de taxis le plus proche?* oo eh luh stah-syohn duh tahks-ee luh plew prohsh
Would you please hail me a cab?	*Pourriez-vous héler un taxi pour moi?* poo-ryay voo ay-lay uhN tahk-see
I want to go … .	*Je voudrais aller … .* zhuh voo-dreh ah-lay ah)
How much is it to go … ?	*C'est combien pour aller … ?* seh kohN-byaN poor ah-lay ah
Stop here please.	*Arrêtez ici s'il vous plaît.* ah-ray-tay ee-see seel voo pleh
Wait for me please.	*Attendez-moi s'il vous plaît.* ah-tahN-day mwah seel voo pleh
How much do I owe you?	*Je vous dois combien?* zhuh voo dwah kohN-byaN

Train Travel

The trains in France are fast and efficient, and they provide service within France as well as to other European countries:

- The TGV (*Train à Grande Vitesse* [traN ah grahnd vee-tehs]) provides high-speed service (up to 200mph [320km] an hour) to hundreds of cities in France as well as other European cities. Reservations are required and should be booked in advance.

- Intercity trains (*trains intercité* [traN aN-tehr-see-tay]) are express trains that travel shorter distances than the TGV but longer distances than local trains. Reservations are required and should be booked in advance.

- TER (*Transport Express Régional* [trahNz-pohr ehks-prehs ray-zhoh-nahl]) provides local train service. No reservations are required and tickets can be purchased in advance.

- Eurostar is a high-speed train that connects France with England, Belgium, and the Netherlands via the Chunnel. Reservations are required, and for the best price, you should book well in advance.

- Thalys (tah-lees) operates high-speed trains that connect Paris with Belgium, the Netherlands, and Germany.

Train tickets can be purchased online, at ticket machines available at train stations, through ticket agents, or by purchasing an Interrail or Eurail Pass.

Where's the nearest train station?	*Où est la gare la plus proche?* oo eh lah gahr lah plew prohsh
Where can I find a schedule?	*Où puis-je trouver un horaire?* oo pweezh troo-vay uhN noh-rehr
I'd like ...	*Je voudrais ...* zhuh voo-dreh ...
a first- (second-) class ticket.	*un billet de première (seconde) classe.* uhN bee-yeh duh pruh-myehr (suh-gohNd) klahs
a one-way ticket.	*un aller simple.* uhN nah-lay saNpl

a round-trip ticket.	*un aller-retour.* uhN nah-lay-ruh-toor
a children's ticket.	*un billet au tarif enfant.* uhN bee-yeh o tah-reef ahN-fahN
a senior ticket.	*un billet au tarif senior.* uhN bee-yeh o tah-reef say-nyohr
a student ticket.	*un billet au tarif étudiant.* uhN bee-yeh o tah-reef ay-tew-dyahN
Are there discounts for children (seniors)?	*Il y a une réduction de prix pour les enfants (les seniors)?* eel yah ewn ray-dewks-yohN duh pree poor lay zahN-fahN (lay say-nyohr)
Are there … passes?	*Il y a des passes … ?* eel yah day pahs
weekly	*hebdomadaires* ehb-doh-mah-dehr
monthly	*mensuelles* mahN-swehl
tourist	*touristiques* too-rees-teek
Is this train a local (express)?	*Est-ce un local (express)?* ehs uhN loh-kahl (ehks-prehss)
Do I have to make a reservation?	*Faut-il réserver?* foo teel ray-zehr-vay
Do I have to change trains? Where?	*Dois-je changer de train? Où?* dwahzh shahN-zhay duh traN oo
At what time does the train leave (arrive)?	*Le train part (arrive) à quelle heure?* luh traN pahr (ah-reev) ah kehl uhr
Will the train arrive on time (late)?	*Le train arrive à l'heure (en retard)?* luh traN ah-reev ah luhr (ahN ruh-tahr)
From what platform does it leave?	*De quel quai part-il?* duh kehl keh pahr-teel

continues

Is there a dining car? Where?	*Il y a un wagon-restaurant?* *Où?* eel yah uhN vah-gohN-reh- stoh-rahN oo
Is there a (non-) smoking car?	*Il y a une voiture (non-)* *fumeurs?* eel yah ewn vwah-tewr (nohN-) few-muhr

Car Travel

I'd like to rent …	*Je voudrais louer …* zhuh voo-dreh loo-ay
a car.	*une voiture.* ewn vwah-tewr
a 4-wheel drive.	*un quatre-quatre.* uhN kahtr-kahtr
a minivan.	*un minivan.* uhN mee-nee-vahn
a motorcycle.	*une motocyclette.* ewn moh-toh-see-kleht
an SUV.	*un SIV.* uhN ehs-ew-vay
an RV.	*un camping-car.* uhN kahN-peeng-kahr
How much does it cost per day (per week) (per kilometer)?	*Quel est le tarif à la journée (à la semaine) (au kilomètre)?* kehl eh luh tah-reef ah lah zhoor-nay (ah lah suh-mehn) (o kee-loh-mehtr)
Can I get unlimited mileage?	*Puis-je obtenir un kilométrage illimité?* pweezh ohp-tuh-neer uhN kee-loh-may-trahzh ee-lee-mee-tay
Does the car have … ?	*La voiture a … ?* lah vwah-tewr ah
ABS	*le freinage anti-blocage* luh freh-nahzh ahN-tee-bloh-kahzh

airbags (passenger side)	*des airbags (côté passager)* day zehr-bahg (ko-tay pah-sah-zhay)
automatic transmission	*la transmission automatique* lah trahNz-mee-syohN o-toh-mah-teek
Bluetooth	*Bluetooth* bloo-toos
GPS	*GPS* zhay-pay-ehs
manual transmission	*la transmission manuelle* lah trahZ-mee-syohN mah-nwehl
power mirrors	*des miroirs électriques* day mee-rwahr ay-lehk-treek
power steering	*la direction assistée* lah dee-rehk-syohN ah-sees-tay
power windows	*des vitres automatiques* day veetr o-toh-mah-teek
How much is the insurance?	*Combien coûte l'assurance?* kohN-byaN koot lah-sew-rahNs
Is the gas included?	*L'essence est comprise?* leh-sahNs eh kohN-preez
Is the mileage included?	*Le kilométrage est compris?* luh kee-loh-may-trahzh eh kohN-pree
What kind of gas does it take?	*La voiture prend quel type d'essence?* lah vwah-tewr prahN kehl teep deh-sahNs
What's the speed limit?	*Quelle est la limite de vitesse?* kehl eh lah lee-meet duh vee-tehs
Do you sell maps (city street maps)?	*Vendez-vous des cartes (plans de la ville)?* vahN-day-voo day kahrt (plahN duh lah veel)

continues

I'd like to return the car to another city.	*Je voudrais rendre la voiture dans une autre ville.* zhuh voo-dreh rahNdr lah vwah-tewr dahN zewn otr veel
What's the charge to drop off the car in another city?	*Combien ça coûte déposer la voiture dans une autre ville?* kohN-byaN sah koot day-po-zay lah vwah-tewr dahN zewn otr veel
Do you accept credit cards? Which ones?	*Acceptez-vous les cartes de crédit? Lesquelles?* ahk-sehp-tay voo lay kahrt duh kray-dee lay-kehl
Do you need my credit card?	*Avez-vous besoin de ma carte de crédit?* ah-vay voo buh-zwaN duh mah kahrt duh kray-dee
Here it is.	*La voilà.* la vwah-lah

When you rent a car in France, make sure it has a jack (*un cric* [uhN kreek]) and a spare tire (*un pneu de secours* [uhN pnuh duh suh-koor]).

Distance is measured in kilometers. One kilometer is the equivalent of .62 miles.

Car Problems

My car broke down.	*Ma voiture est en panne.* mah vwah-tewr eh tahN pahn
Where's the nearest gas station?	*Où est la station-service la plus proche?* oo eh lah stah-syohN-sehr-vees lah plew prohsh
I have a flat tire.	*J'ai un pneu à plat.* zhay uhN pnuh ah plah
The battery died.	*La batterie est morte.* lah bah-tree eh mohrt
The car won't start.	*La voiture ne démarre pas.* lah vwah-tewr nuh day-mahr pah

The car is overheating.	*Le moteur chauffe.* luh moh-tuhr shof
Water is leaking from the radiator.	*Le radiateur coule.* luh rahd-yah-tuhr kool
Oil is leaking from the engine.	*De l'huile fuit du moteur.* duh lweel fwee dew moh-tuhr
I locked the keys.	*J'ai enfermé les clés à l'intérieur.* zhay ahN-fehr-may lay klay ah laN-tay-ryuhr
I've had an accident.	*J'ai eu un accident.* zhay ew uhN nahk-see-dahN
Can you please help me?	*Pourriez-vous m'aider?* poo-ryay-voo may-day
Can you please tow (fix) my car?	*Pourriez-vous remorquer (réparer) ma voiture?* poo-ryay-voo ruh-mohr-kay (ray-pah-ray) mah vwah-tewr
How long will it take?	*Ça va prendre combien de temps?* sah vah prahNdr kohN-byaN duh tahN
When will it be ready?	*Quand sera-t-elle prête?* kahN suh-rah-tehl preht
How much do I owe you?	*Je vous dois combien?* zhuh voo dwah kohN-byaN

Getting Directions

Continue ...	*Continuez ...* kohN-tee-new-ay
Cross ...	*Traversez ...* trah-vehr-say
Follow ...	*Suivez ...* swee-vay
Go down ...	*Descendez ...* day-sahN-day
Go up ...	*Montez ...* mohN-tay

continues

Go ...	*Allez ...* ah-lay
Pass ...	*Passez ...* pah-say
Take ...	*Prenez ...* pruh-nay
Turn ...	*Tournez ...* toor-nay
Walk ...	*Marchez ...* mahr-shay
It's	*Il (Elle) est .... .* eel (ehl) eh
above ...	*au dessus de* *(du, de la, de l')* ... o duh-sew duh (dew, duh la, duhl)
at ...	*à (au, à la, à l')* ... ah (o, ah lah, ahl)
behind ...	*derrière (le, la, l', les)* ... deh-ryehr (luh, lah, l, lay)
far (from) ...	*loin (de [du, de la, de l'])* ... lwaN duh (dew, duh la, duhl)
from ...	*de (du, de la, de l')* ... duh (dew, duh la, duhl)
in ...	*dans (le, la, l', les)* ... dahN (luh, lah, l, lay)
in front of ...	*devant (le, la, l', les)* ... duh-vahN (luh, lah, l, lay)
near (to) ...	*près (de [du, de la, de l'])* ... preh duh (dew, duh la, duhl)
next to ...	*à côté de (du, de la, de l')* ... ah ko-tay duh (dew, duh la, duhl)
opposite ...	*en face de (du, de la, de l')* ... ahN fahs duh (dew, duh la, duhl)

to ...	*à (au, à la, à l')* ... ah (o, ah la, ahl)
toward ...	*vers (le, la, l', les)* ... vehr (luh, lah, l, lay)
to the north	*au nord* o nohr
to the east	*à l'est* ah lehst
to the south	*au sud* o sewd
to the west	*à l'ouest* ah lwehst
to the right	*à droite* ah drwaht
to the left	*à gauche* ah gosh

It's two blocks from here (in that direction).

Il (Elle) est à deux pâtés de maisons d'ici (dans cette direction).
eel (ehl) eh tah duh pah-tay duh meh-zohN dee-see (dahN seht dee-rehk-syohN)

Note that *à* + *le* becomes *au* and *de* + *le* becomes *du*.

It's to the south.

Il est au sud.
eel eh to sewd

It's next to the theater.

Il est à côté du théâtre.
eel eh tah ko-tay dew tay-ahtr

Chapter 8

Accommodations

When it comes to accommodations, are the bare
necessities acceptable or do you prefer total luxury?
Perhaps something in between the two would suit
your needs? Whatever your personal requirements,
this chapter will help you get the room and services
you desire.

Hotel Accommodations

Possible places to stay in France include:

- *Un hôtel* (uhN no-tehl) is usually rated by the France Tourism Development Agency (Atout France), which provides a star system from inexpensive (one star) to very expensive (five stars). The accommodations and amenities the hotel offers—as well as its location—determine the number of stars it receives. Displayed prices are all-inclusive.

- *Un motel* (uhN mo-tehl) can usually be found near an airport, near main roads in rural areas, and outside large cities.

- *Une pension* (ewn pahN-syohN) is similar to a rooming house, where guests pay for a room and all or some of their meals. These cozy, comfortable establishments provide anything from the bare minimum to the very luxurious.

- *Une auberge* (ewn o-behrzh) is a roadside inn that generally provides services for people traveling by car.

- *Une auberge de jeunesse* (ewn o-behrzh duh zhuh-nehs) is a youth hostel that provides a dormitory setting.

- *Une chambre d'hôtes* (ewn shahNbr dot) is a bed-and-breakfast (usually in the proprietor's house) that's maintained by local families in small towns and villages.

- *Un gîte rural* (uhN zheet rew-rahl) is a private home or apartment that's for rent.

You can also rent (*louer* [loo-ay]) the following.

- *Une maison* (ewn meh-zohN): a house

- *Un appartement* (uhN nah-pahr-tuh-mahN): an apartment

- *Un condo* (uhN kohN-do): a condo

- *Une cabane* (ewn kah-bahn): a cabin

The ground floor is *le rez-de-chaussée* (luh rayd sho-say, abbreviated *rez-de-ch*) and the basement is *le sous-sol* (luh soo-sohl, abbreviated *s-s*). Thus, the first floor is really on the second floor.

Tipping

Hotel bills generally include a service charge of 15%. However, it's customary to tip the bellhop who takes care of your luggage, the housekeeper, room service, and a doorperson who calls for a taxi. If a concierge is present and performs special services—making restaurant reservations, procuring tickets, etc.—a tip is warranted.

Amenities, Facilities & Services

Is (Are) there … ?	*Il y a … ?* eel yah
access for people with disabilities	*un accès pour les personnes handicapées* uhN nahks-eh poor lay pehr-sohn ahN-dee-kah-pay
access for wheelchairs	*un accès pour les chaises roulantes* uhN nahks-eh poor lay shez roo-lahNt

continues

air-conditioning	*la climatisation* lah klee-mah-tee-zah-syohN
babysitting services	*la garde d'enfants* lah gahrd dahN-fahN
a bar	*un bar* uhN bahr
a bellhop	*un chasseur* uhN shah-suhr
a beauty salon	*un salon de beauté* uhN sah-lohN duh bo-tay
a bridal suite	*une suite nuptiale* ewn sweet newp-syahl
a business center	*un centre d'affaires* uhN sahNtr dah-fehr
a coffee machine	*une machine à café* ewn mah-sheen ah kah-feh
a concierge	*un (une) concierge* uhN (ewn) kohN-syehrzh
a crib	*un berceau* uhN behr-so
a door attendant	*un portier* uhN pohr-tyay
a dry-cleaning service	*le service de nettoyage à sec* luh sehr-vees duh neh-twah-yahzh ah sehk
an elevator	*un ascenseur* uhN nah-sahN-suhr
a fitness center	*une salle de gym* ewn sahl duh zheem
a gift shop	*une boutique de cadeaux* ewn boo-teek duh kah-do
housekeeping	*l'entretien* lahNtr-tyaN
an ice maker	*un distributeur de glaçons* uhN dees-tree-bew-tuhr duh glah-sohN
internet service	*le service internet* luh sehr-vees aN-tehr-neht

a laundry	*une blanchisserie*
	ewn blahN-shees-ree
a minibar	*un minibar*
	uhN mee-nee-bahr
pay-per-view television	*la télévision à la carte*
	lah tay-lay-vee-zyohN ah
	lah kahrt
a porter	*un bagagiste*
	uhN bah-gah-zheest
a restaurant	*un restaurant*
	uhN rehs-toh-rahN
room service	*le service de chambre*
	luh sehr-vees duh shahNbr
a safe	*un coffre-fort*
	uhN kohfr-fohr
services for people	*des services pour les*
with disabilities	*personnes handicapées*
	day sehr-vees poor lay
	pehr-sohn ahN-dee-kah-pay
shuttle service	*le service de navette*
	luh sehr-vees duh nah-veht
a sofa bed	*un canapé-lit*
	uhN kah-nah-pay-lee
a spa	*un spa*
	uhN spah
a swimming pool	*une piscine (couverte)*
(indoor)	ewn pee-seen (koo-vehrt)
a TV (with cable)	*une télévision (par câble)*
	ewn tay-lay-vee-zyohN
	(pahr kahbl)
valet parking	*l'attendance du garage*
	lah-tahN-dahNs dew
	gah-rahzh
vending machines	*les distributeurs*
	automatiques
	lay dees-tree-bew-tuhr
	o-toh-mah-teek
a Wi-Fi network	*un réseau Wi-Fi*
	uhN ray-zo wee-fee

Special Amenities

At what time does the ... open (close)?	*Le (la) ... ouvre (ferme) à quelle heure?* luh (lah) ... oo-vruh (fehrm) ah kehl uhr
I'd like an appointment for ... at ... o'clock.	*Je voudrais un rendez-vous pour ... à ... heure(s).* zhuh voo-dreh uhN rahN-day voo pour ... ah ... uhr
a facial	*un soin de visage* uhN swaN duh vee-zahzh
a haircut	*une coupe de cheveux* ewn koop duh shuh-vuh
a (French) manicure	*une manucure (française)* ewn mah-new-kewr (frahN-sehz)
a massage	*un massage* uhN mah-sahzh
a pedicure	*une pédicure* ewn pay-dee-kewr
a shampoo	*un shampooing* uhN shahN-pwaN
a shave	*un rasage* uhN rah-zahzh
a waxing	*une épilation à la cire* ewn ay-pee-lah-syohN ah lah seer
Please wash and blow-dry my hair.	*Lavez et séchez mes cheveux s'il vous plaît.* lah-vay ay say-shay may shuh-vuh seel voo pleh
How much does it cost?	*Ça coûte combien?* sah koot kohN-byaN
Is the tip included?	*Le service est compris?* luh sehr-vees eh kohN-pree
Is there a fee to use the gym?	*Il y a des frais pour utiliser la salle de gym?* eel yah day freh poor oo-tee-lee-zay lah sahl duh zheem

How much is it?	*C'est combien?* seh kohN-byaN
Is there … ?	*Il y a … ?* eel yah
a pool	*une piscine* ewn pee-seen
a sauna	*un sauna* uhN so-nah
a steam room	*une chambre à vapeur* ewn shahNbr ah vah-puhr
a jacuzzi	*un jacuzzi* uhN zhah-kew-zee

Accessibility

We need special accommodations.	*Nous avons besoin de logement spécial.* noo zah-vohN buh-zwaN duh lohzh-mahN spay-syahl
What services do you have for people with disabilities?	*Quels services offrez vous pour les personnes handicapées?* kehl sehr-vees oh-fray voo poor lay pehr-sohn ahN-dee-kah-pay
Are there ramps?	*Il y a des rampes d'accèes?* eel yah des rahmp dahks-eh
Are the signs written in Braille?	*Les pancartes sont-elles écrites en Braille?* lay pahN-kahrt sohN-tehl ay-kreet ahN brah-y
Can you provide a wheelchair (walker)?	*Pourriez-vous fournir une chaise roulante (un déambulateur)?* poo-ryay-voo foor-neer ewn shehz roo-lahNt (uhN day-ahN-bew-lah-tuhr)
Is there a doctor (dentist) available?	*Il y a un(e) docteur (dentiste) à notre disposition?* eel yah uhN (ewn) dohk-tuhr (dahN-teest) ah nohtr dees-po-zee-syohN

continues

Is there a ground-floor (first-floor) room available?	*Il y a une chambre au rez-de-chaussée (au premier étage)?* eel yah ewn shahNbr o rayd sho-say (o pruh-myay ay-tahzh)
Are there toilet facilities accessible for people with disabilities?	*Il y a des accessible aux personnes handicapées?* eel yah day twah-leht ahk-seh-seebl o pehr-sohn ahN-dee-kah-pay
Are there bathrooms on the ground floor?	*Il y a des toilettes au rez-de-chaussée?* eel yah day twah-leht o rayd-sho-say
Are there bars in the bathroom (the shower)?	*Il y a des barres dans les toilettes (la douche)?* eel yah day bahr dahN lay twah-leht (lah doosh)
Is there a refrigerator (a freezer) in the room?	*Il y a un réfrigérateur (un congélateur) dans la chambre?* eel yah uhN ray-free-zhay-rah-tuhr (uhN kohN-zhay-lah-tuhr) dahN lah shahNbr
Do you have closed-captioned TV?	*Avez-vous l'option sous-titres sur les télévisions?* ah-vay-voo lohp-syohN soo-teetr sewr lay tay-lay-vee-zyohN
Is there accessible (disability) parking?	*Il y a un parking pour les personnes handicapées?* eel yah uhN pahr-keeng poor lay pehr-sohn ahN-dee-kah-pay
Where can I get a disability parking permit?	*Où puis-je obtenir un permis de parking pour les personnes handicapées?* oo pweezh ohp-tuh-neer uhN pehr-mee duh pahr-keeng poor lay pehr-sohn ahN-dee-kah-pay
Where's a compound pharmacy?	*Où se trouve une pharmacie réalisant des préparations magistrales?* oo suh troov ewn fahr-mah-see ray-ah-lee-zahN day pray-pah-rah-syohN mah-zhees-trahl

Where's an all-night pharmacy?	*Où se trouve une pharmacie de ouverte la nuit?* oo suh troov ewn fahr-mah-see duh gahrd oo-vehrt lah nwee
Where can I buy batteries for my hearing aid?	*Où puis-je acheter des piles pour mon appareil auditif?* oo pweezh ahsh-tay day peel poor mohN nah-pah-reh-y o-dee-teef
Does anyone know American Sign Language?	*Quelqu'un connaît la langue des signes américaine?* kehl-kuhN koh-neh lah lahng day see-nyuh ah-may-ree-kehn

Checking In

I have a (don't have a) reservation.	*J'ai une (Je n'ai pas de) réservation.* zhay ewn (zhuh nay pah duh) ray-zehr-vah-syohN
Are there any available rooms?	*Il y a des chambres disponibles?* eel yah day shahNbr dees-poh-neebl
I'd like ...	*Je voudrais ...* zhuh voo-dreh
a single (double) room.	*une chambre à un (deux) lit(s).* ewn shahNbr ah uhN (duh) lee
adjoining rooms.	*des chambres attenantes.* day shahNbr aht-nahNt
a non-adjoining room.	*une chambre non-attenante à une autre.* ewn shahNbr nohN-aht-nahNt ah ewn otr
I'd like a room (an apartment) ...	*Je voudrais une chambre (un appartement) ...* zhuh voo-dreh ewn shahNbr (uhN nah-pahr-tuh-mahN)
on the ground floor.	*au rez-de-chaussée.* o rayd-sho-say

continues

facing the garden.	*qui donne sur le jardin.* kee dohn sewr luh zhahr-dahN
facing the courtyard.	*qui donne sur la cour.* kee dohn sewr lah koor
(not) facing the street.	*qui (ne) donne (pas) sur la rue.* kee (nuh) dohn (pah) sewr lah rew
with a balcony.	*avec balcon.* ah-vehk bahl-kohN
that's accessible for people with disabilities.	*accessible aux personnes handicapées.* ahks-eh-seebl o pehr-sohn ahN-dee-kah-pay
How much is it per night (week) (month)?	*C'est combien par nuit (semaine) (mois)?* seh kohN-byaN pahr nwee (suh-mehn) (mwah)
I (we) will be staying one night (a week) (two weeks).	*Je reste (Nous restons) une nuit (une semaine) (deux semaines).* zhuh rehst (noo rehs-tohN) ewn nwee (ewn suh-mehn) (duh suh-mehn)
Is breakfast included?	*Le petit déjeuner est compris?* luh puh-tee day-zhuh-nay eh kohN-pree
How much do you charge for children?	*C'est combien pour les enfants?* seh kohN-byaN poor lay zahN-fahN
Could you put a crib (another bed) in the room?	*Pourriez-vous mettre un berceau (un autre lit) dans la chambre?* poor-yay-voo mehtr uhN behr-so (uhN notr lee) dahN lah shahNbr
Is there a discount for seniors (children)?	*Il y a une réduction de prix pour les seniors (les enfants)?* eel yah ewn ray-dewks-yohN duh pree poor lay say-nyohr (lay zahN-fahN)

Is there a charge for the internet (Wi-Fi)?	*Il y a un tarif pour le service internet (Wi-Fi)?* eel yah uhN tah-reef poor luh sehr-vees aN-tehr-neht (wee-fee)
What floor is the room on?	*La chambre est à quel étage?* lah shahNbr eh tah kehl ay-tahzh
What's the room number?	*Quel est le numéro de la chambre?* kehl eh luh new-may-ro duh lah shahNbr
May I see the room?	*Puis-je voir la chambre?* pweezh vwahr lah shahNbr
Is everything included?	*Tout est compris?* too teh kohN-pree
I like (don't like) the room.	*J'aime (Je n'aime pas) la chambre.* zhehm (zhuh nehm pah) lah shahNbr
May I see another room?	*Puis-je voir une autre chambre?* pweezh vwahr ewn otr shahNbr
Is there something … ?	*Avez-vous quelque chose de … ?* ah-vay voo kehl-kuh shoz duh
better	*meilleur* meh-yuhr
bigger	*plus grand* plew grahN
smaller	*plus petit* plew puh-tee
cheaper	*meilleur marché* meh-yuhr mahr-shay
quieter	*plus silencieux* plew see-lahN-syuh
May I have the key?	*Puis-je avoir la clé?* pweezh ah-vwahr lah klay
Where's the elevator?	*Où est l'ascenseur?* oo eh lah-sahN-suhr

continues

Where are the emergency exits?	*Où sont les sorties de secours?* oo sohN lay sohr-tee duh suh-koor
Can somebody help me with my luggage?	*Quelqu'un peut m'aider avec mes bagages?* kehl-kuhn puh may-day ah-vehk may bah-gahzh
At what time do I have to check out?	*À quelle heure faut-il régler sa note?* ah kehl uhr fo-teel ray-glay sah noht
Is there automatic checkout?	*Peut-on régler sa note automatiquement?* puh-tohN ray-glay sah noht o-toh-mah-teek-mahN

Room Needs

I (We) need ...	*Il me (nous) faut ...* eel muh (noo) fo
an adaptor.	*un adapteur.* uhN ah-dahp-tuhr
an ashtray.	*un cendrier.* uhN sahN-dree-yay
a bar of soap.	*une savonnette.* ewn sah-voh-neht
a blanket.	*une couvrture.* ewn koo-vehr-tewr
clean sheets.	*des draps propres.* day drah prohpr
conditioner (hair).	*de l'après-shampooing.* duh lah-preh shahN-pwaN
a hair dryer.	*un sèche-cheveux.* uhN sehsh-shuh-vuh
hangers.	*des cintres.* day saNtr
ice cubes.	*des glaçons.* day glah-sohN
a key.	*une clé.* ewn klay

a king-sized bed.	*un lit king-size.* uhN lee keeng-size
mineral water.	*de l'eau minérale.* duh lo mee-nay-rahl
mouthwash.	*du bain de bouche.* dew baN duh boosh
a pillow.	*un oreiller.* uhN noh-reh-yay
shampoo.	*du shampooing.* dew shahN-pwaN
a shower cap.	*un bonnet de douche.* uhN boh-neh duh doosh
tissues.	*des mouchoirs en papier.* day moo-shwahr ahN pahp-yay
toilet paper.	*du papier hygiénique.* dew pah-pyay ee-zhyay-neek
towels.	*des serviettes.* day sehr-vyeht
a transformer.	*un transformateur.* uhN trahNs-fohr-mah-tuhr

Breakfast

Where's the dining room?	*Où est la salle à manger?* oo eh lah sahl ah mahN-zhay
Is there a buffet?	*Il y a un buffet?* eel yah uhN bew-feh
What's the number for room service?	*Quel est le numéro pour le service de chambre?* kehl eh luh new-may-ro poor luh sehr-vees duh shahNbr
I'd like (We'd like) ...	*Je voudrais (Nous voudrions) ...* zhuh voo-dreh (noo voo-dree-yohN)
bacon.	*du bacon.* dew bay-kohN

continues

bread.	*du pain.* dew paN
butter.	*du beurre.* dew buhr
cereal.	*des céréales.* day say-ray-ahl
coffee (decaffeinated) (black).	*du café (déscaféiné) (noir).* dew kah-fay (day-kah-fay-ee-nay) (nwahr)
cream.	*de la crème.* duh lah krehm
... eggs.	*des œufs ...* day zuh
fried	*frits.* free
hard-boiled	*durs.* dewr
poached	*pochés.* poh-shay
scrambled	*brouillés.* broo-yay
soft-boiled	*mollets (à la coque).* moh-leh (ah lah kohk)
French toast.	*du pain perdu.* dew paN pehr-dew
fresh fruit.	*des fruits frais.* day frwee freh
hot chocolate.	*du chocolat.* dew shoh-koh-lah
jam.	*de la confiture.* duh lah kohN-fee-tewr
... juice.	*du jus ... .* dew zhew
apple	*de pomme* duh pohm
grape	*de raisin* de reh-zaN
grapefruit	*de pamplemousse* duh pahN-pluh-moos

orange	*d'orange* doh-rahNzh
pineapple	*d'ananas* dah-nah-nah
a lemon.	*un citron.* uhN see-trohN
margarine.	*de la margarine.* duh lah mahr-gah-reen
milk.	*du lait.* dew leh
mineral water (flat) (bubbly).	*de l'eau minérale (plate)* *(gazeuse).* duh lo mee-nay-rahl (plaht) (gah-zuhz)
oatmeal.	*de la bouillie d'avoine.* duh la boo-yee dah-vwahn
an omelet.	*une omelette.* ewn ohm-leht
pancakes.	*des crêpes.* day krehp
pastries.	*des pâtisseries.* day pah-tees-ree
rolls.	*des petits pains.* day puh-tee paN
sausages.	*des saucisses.* day so-sees
sugar.	*du sucre.* dew sewkr
tea (decaffeinated).	*du thé (décaféiné).* dew tay (day-kah-fay-ee-nay)
toast.	*du pain grillé.* dew paN gree-yay

Child Care

To be polite, use *s'il vous plaît* (seel voo pleh) to express "please" either before or after asking someone to perform a service for you.

Give him/her (them) breakfast (lunch) (dinner).	*Donnez-lui (-leur) le petit déjeuner (le déjeuner) (le dîner).* doh-nay lwee (luhr) luh puh-tee day-zhuh-nay (luh day-zhuh-nay) (luh dee-nay)
Feed him/her (them) at … o'clock.	*Donnez-lui (-leur) à manger à … heures.* doh-nay lwee (luhr) ah mahN-zhay ah … uhr
He (She) doesn't eat … .	*Il (Elle) ne mange pas de … .* eel (ehl) nuh mahNzh pah duh
Bathe him/her at … o'clock (in the morning) (evening).	*Donnez-lui un bain à … heures (du matin) (du soir).* doh-nay-lwee uhN baN à … uhr (dew mah-taN) (dew swahr)
He (She) prefers a shower.	*Il (Elle) préfère une douche.* eel (ehl) pray-fehr ewn doosh
Don't allow the children …	*Ne permettez pas aux enfants de …* nuh pehr-meh-tay pah zo zahN-fahN duh
to eat sweets.	*manger de bonbons.* mahN-zhay duh bohN-bohN
to drink soda.	*boire de soda.* bwahr duh soh-dah
to talk too long on their cell phone.	*parler trop longtemps au portable (mobile).* pahr-lay tro lohN-tahN o pohr-tahbl (moh-beel)
to watch TV.	*regarder la télévision.* ruh-gahr-day lah tay-lay-vee-zyohN

Limit screen time to … minutes.	*Limitez le temps d'écran à … minutes.* lee-mee-tay luh tahN day-krahN ah … mee-newt
Nap time is … o'clock.	*… heure(s) est l'heure de sieste.* … uhr eh luhr duh see-ehst
Bedtime is … o'clock.	*… heures est l'heure du coucher.* … uhr eh luhr dew koo-shay
If there's a problem, call me.	*S'il y a un problème, téléphonez-moi.* seel yah uhN proh-blehm tay-lay-fohnay-mwah

Housekeeping Services

Could you … ?	*Pourriez-vous … ?* poo-ryay-voo
clean the room now (later)	*nettoyer la chambre maintenant (plus tard)* neh-twah-yah lah shahNbr maNt-nahN (plew tahr)
dust	*enlever la poussière* ahN-lvay lah poo-syehr
vacuum	*passer l'aspirateur* pah-say lahs-pee-rah-tuhr
wash the dishes	*faire la vaisselle* fehr lah veh-sehl
load (unload) (turn on) the dishwasher	*charger (décharger) (allumer) le lave-vaisselle* shahr-zhay (day-shahr-zhay) (ah-lew-may) luh lahv-veh-sehl
do the laundry	*faire la lessive* fehr lah leh-seev
(not) use bleach (fabric softener)	*(ne pas) utiliser l'eau de javel (adoucissant)* (nuh pahz) oo-tee-lee-zay lo duh zhah-vehl (ah-doo-see-sahN)

continues

change the sheets	*changer les draps* shahN-zhay lay drah
iron the clothes	*repasser les vêtements* ruh-pah-say lay veht-mahN
empty the garbage	*vider les ordures* vee-day lay zohr-dewr
take out the garbage	*sortir les poubelles* sohr-teer lay poo-behl
water the plants	*arroser les plantes* ah-ro-zay lay plahNt

Concierge Services

Can I get a room upgrade?	*Puis-je obtenir un* *surclassement de chambre?* pweezh ohp-tuh-neer uhN sewr-klahs-mahN duh shahNbr
Can you hail a cab (a rideshare)?	*Pourriez-vous héler un taxi* *(un covoiturage)?* poo-ryay-voo ay-lay uhN tahks-ee (uhN ko-vwah-tew-rahzh)
What can my children do for fun?	*Que peuvent faire mes* *enfants pour s'amuser?* kuh puhv fehr may zahN-fahN poor sah-mew-zay
Can you help me get a babysitter?	*Pourriez-vous m'aider* *à avoir un baby-sitter?* poo-ryay-voo may-day ah ah-vwahr uhN babysitter
Can you help me (help us) celebrate … ?	*Pourriez-vous m'aider* *(nous aider) à célébrer … ?* poo-ryay voo may-day (noo zay-day) ah say-lay-bray
a birthday	*un anniversaire* uhN nah-nee-vehr-sehr
an engagement	*des fiançailles* day fee-ahN-sah-y
a special wedding anniversary	*un anniversaire* *de mariage spécial* uhN nah-nee-vehr-sehr duh mah-ryahzh spay-syahl

a special occasion	*une occasion spéciale* ewn noh-kah-zyohN spay-syahl
a wedding	*un mariage* uhN mah-ryahzh
Can you recommend me (us) ... ?	*Pourriez-vous me (nous) recommander ... ?* poo-ryay-voo muh (noo) ruh-koh-mahN-day
a nightclub	*une boîte de nuit* ewn bwaht duh nwee
a (child-friendly restaurant	*un restaurant (adapté aux enfants)* uhN rehs-toh-rahN (ah-dahp-tay o zahN-fahN)
Can you make a reservation for me (us)?	*Pourriez-vous me (nous) faire une réservation?* poo-ryay-voo muh (noo) fehr ewn ray-zehr-vah-syohN
Can you get me (us) tickets for ... ?	*Pourriez-vous obtenir des billets pour moi (nous) pour ... ?* poo-ryay-voo zohp-tuh-neer day bee-yeh poor mwah (noo) poor
this concert	*ce concert* suh kohN-sehr
this exhibition	*cette exposition* seht ehks-poh-zee-syohN
this play	*cette pièce* seht pyehs
this show	*ce spectacle* suh spehk-tahkl
this sporting event	*cet événement sportif* seht ay-vayn-mahN spohr-teef
Can you recommend me (us) a reliable tour guide?	*Pourriez-vous me (nous) recommander un(e) guide touristique fiable?* poo-ryay-voo muh (noo) ruh-koh-mahN-day uhN (ewn) geed too-rees-teek fee-ahbl

continues

Where can I buy ... ?	*Où puis-je acheter ... ?* oo pweez ahsh-tay
clothing	*des vêtements* day veht-mahN
gifts	*des cadeaux* day kah-do
souvenirs	*des souvenirs* day soo-vneer
handicrafts	*des artisanats* day zahr-tee-zah-nah
jewelry	*des bijoux* day bee-zhoo
a phone charger	*un chargeur de portable* *(mobile)* uhN shahr-zhuhr duh pohr-tahbl (moh-beel)
Could you please print out my (our) boarding pass(es)?	*Pourriez-vous imprimer* *ma (nos) carte(s)* *d'embarquement?* poo-ryay-voo zaN-pree-may mah (noh) kahrt dahN-bahrk- mahN

Problems, Complaints & Concerns

There's a problem.	*Il y a un problème.* eel yah uhN proh-blehm
There's no ...	*Il n'y a pas de (d') ...* eel nyah pah duh (d)
cold water.	*eau froide.* o frwahd
electricity.	*électricité.* ay-lehk-tree-see-tay
heat.	*chauffage.* sho-fahzh
hot water.	*eau chaude.* o shod

running water.	*eau courante.* o koo-rahNt
The ... doesn't work.	*... ne marche pas.* ... nuh mahrsh pah
air-conditioning	*La climatisation ...* lah klee-mah-tee-zah-syohN
cable	*La télévision par câble ...* lah tay-lay-vee-zyohN pahr kahbl
elevator	*L'ascenseur ...* lah-sahN-suhr
fan	*Le ventilateur ...* luh vahN-tee-lah-tuhr
faucet	*Le robinet ...* luh roh-bee-neh
internet	*La service internet ...* lah sehr-vees aN-tehr-neht
lamp (light)	*La lampe ...* lah lahNp
outlet	*La prise de courant ...* lah preez duh koo-rahN
radio	*La radio ...* lah rahd-yo
refrigerator	*Le réfrigérateur ...* luh ray-free-zhay-rah-tuhr
safe	*Le coffre-fort ...* luh kohfr-fohr
switch	*L'interrupteur ...* laN-tay-rewp-tuhr
television	*La télévision ...* lah tay-lay-vee-zyohN
Wi-Fi	*Le Wi-Fi ...* luh wee-fee
Could you fix it as soon as possible?	*Pourriez-vous le (la) réparer aussitôt que possible?* poo-ryay voo luh (lah) ray-pah-ray o-see-to kuh poh-seebl

continues

We need an exterminator.	*Nous avons besoin d'un exterminateur.* noo zah-vohN buh-zwaN duhN nehks-tehr-mee-nah-tuhr
There are ...	*Il y a ...* eel yah
bedbugs.	*des punaises de lit.* day pew-nehz duh lee
bees.	*des abeilles.* day zah-beh-y
insects.	*des insectes.* day zahN-sehkt
mice.	*des souris.* day soo-ree
Can I block certain television channels?	*Puis-je bloquer certaines chaînes de télévision?* pweezh bloh-kay sehr-tehn shehn duh tay-lay-vee-zyohN

Checking Out

I'd like the bill please.	*Je voudrais la note s'il vous plaît.* zhuh voo-dreh lah noht see voo pleh
Do you accept credit cards? Which ones?	*Acceptez-vous les cartes de crédit? Lesquelles?* ahks-ehp-tay voo lay kahrt duh kray-dee lay-kehl
I think there's a mistake with the bill.	*Je crois qu'il y a une erreur avec la note.* zhuh krwah keel yah ewn eh-ruhr ah-vehk lah noht
I lost the key.	*J'ai perdu la clé.* zhay pehr-dew lah klay
I'll (We'll) be checking out tomorrow.	*Je pars (Nous partons) demain.* zhuh pahr (noo pahr-tohN) duh-maN

Please send up the bellhop. *S'il vous plaît faites monter
le chasseur.*
seel voo pleh feht mohN-tay
luh shah-suhr

Other Accommodations

I'd like to rent ... *Je voudrais louer ...*
zhuh voo-dreh loo-ay

an apartment. *un appartement.*
uhN nah-pahr-tuh-mahN

a cabin. *une cabane.*
ewn kah-bahn

a condo. *un condo.*
uhN kohN-do

a house. *une maison.*
ewn meh-zohN

I'd like to stay in *Je voudrais rester dans*
a bed-and-breakfast. *une chambre d'hôtes.*
zhuh voo-dreh rehs-tay dahN
zewn shahNbr dot

How much does it cost *Ça coûte combien par nuit*
per day (week) (month)? *(semaine) (mois)?*
sah koot kohN-byaN pahr
nwee (suh-mehn) (mwah)

Is gas (heat) included? *Le gaz (Le chauffage)
est compris?*
luh gahz (luh sho-fahzh) eh
kohN-pree

Is air-conditioning *La climatisation (L'électricité)*
(electricity) included? *est comprise?*
lah klee-mah-tee-zah-syohN
(lay-lehk-tree-see-tay) eh
kohN-preez

How many rooms *Il y a combien de pièces*
(bedrooms) (bathrooms) *(chambres) (salles de bains)?*
are there? eel yah kohN-byaN duh pyehs
(shahNbr) (sahl duh baN)

continues

Can we park our RV at this campsite?	*Pouvons-nous garer notre véhicule dans ce camping?* poo-vohN-noo gah-ray nohtr vay-ee-kewl dahN suh kahN-peeng
How much does it cost per night?	*C'est combien par nuit?* seh kohN-byaN pahr nwee
Is (Are) there … ?	*Il y a … ?* eel yah
cooking facilities	*des équipements de cuisine* day zay-keep-mahN duh kwee-zeen
drinking water	*de l'eau potable* duh lo poh-tahbl
electricity	*de l'électricité* duh lay-lehk-tree-see-tay
a picnic area	*un aire de pique-nique* uhN nehr duh peek-neek
a playground	*un terrain de jeu* uhN teh-raN duh zhuh
showers	*des douches* day doosh
toilet facilities	*des sanitaires* day sah-nee-tehr

Chapter 9

Food

Whether you want to make reservations for a fancy four-star restaurant or just stop by a local *charcuterie* (shahr-kew-tree; deli) to pick up a bite to tide you over, you need to know how to ask for the foods you want and how to refuse those that don't have any appeal. You'll also want to ensure you order the proper quantity. This chapter will help you with all these situations.

Meals

The French-speaking world boasts a diversified cuisine influenced by its varied cultures. Because each region of France and each French-speaking country has its own specialties, the following phrases are general and intended to help you navigate a menu no matter where you travel.

- **Breakfast:** *Le petit déjeuner* (luh puh-tee day-zhuh-nay) is much lighter than its American counterpart, typically consisting of coffee with milk or hot chocolate and a croissant or a brioche (sweet roll) with butter or jam. This continental breakfast is what you'll most often be served if breakfast is included in the price of your room.

- **Lunch:** *Le déjeuner* (luh day-zhuh-nay) is considered the main meal of the day and, in fact, might be the same size or larger than dinner. Lunch often includes soup, meat or fish, vegetables, salad, and dessert, and it might last for an hour or more.

- **Dinner:** *Le dîner* (luh dee-nay) tends to be light but can also contain many courses, as with lunch.

At a Restaurant

If you're looking for a place to eat, you can choose from the following.

- *Une auberge* (ewn o-behrzh): an inn

- *Un bistro* (uhN bees-tro): an informal neighborhood pub or tavern

- *Une brasserie* (ewn brahs-ree): a larger café serving quick meals

- *Un cabaret* (uhN kah-bah-reh): a caberet

- *Un café* (uhN kah-fay): a small neighborhood restaurant where residents socialize

- *Une cafétéria* (ewn kah-fay-tay-ryah): a self-service restaurant

- *Une casse-croûte* (ewn kahs-kroot): a restaurant serving sandwiches

- *Une crêperie* (ewn krehp-ree): a stand or restaurant serving crêpes (filled pancakes)

- *Un fast-food* (uhN fahst-food): a fast-food chain restaurant

- *Un restaurant* (uhN rehs-toh-rahN): a family-run or an elegant dining establishment

- *Un self* (uhN sehlf): a self-service restaurant

Making Reservations

Can you recommend me (us) a good ... restaurant ... ?	*Pourriez-vous me (nous) recommandez un bon restaurant ... ?* poo-ryay-voo muh (noo) ruh-koh-mahN-day uhN bohN rehs-toh-rahN
vegetarian	*végétarien* vay-zhay-tah-ryaN
vegan	*végétalien* vay-zhay-tah-lyaN
serving regional dishes	*de cuisine régionale* duh kwee-zeen ray-zhoh-nahl

continues

I'd like to reserve a table ... please.	*Je voudrais réserver une table ... s'il vous plaît.* zhuh voo-dreh ray-zehr-vay ewn tahbl ... seel voo pleh
for this evening	*pour ce soir* poor suh swahr
for tomorrow evening	*pour demain soir* poor duh-maN swahr
for Saturday evening	*pour samedi soir* poor sahm-dee swahr
for two (four) people	*pour deux (quatre) personnes* poor duh (kahtr) pehr-sohn
for 8:30	*à huit heures et demie* ah wee tuhr ay duh-mee
inside	*à l'intérieur* ah laN-tay-ryuhr
outside	*à l'extérieur* ah lehks-tay-ryuhr
on the terrace	*sur la terrasse* sewr lah teh-rahs
in a (quiet) corner	*dans un coin (tranquille)* dahN zuhN kwaN (trahN-keel)
near the window	*près de la fenêtre* preh duh lah fuh-nehtr
far from the door	*loin de la porte* lwaN duh lah pohrt
far from the kitchen	*loin de la cuisine* lwaN duh lah kwee-zeen
Is there a dress code?	*Il y a un code vestimentaire?* eel yah uhN kohd vehs-tee-mahN-tehr
Do I have to wear a dinner jacket (a suit)?	*Dois-je porter un smoking (un costume)?* dwahzh pohr-tay uhN smoh-keeng (uhN kohs-tewm)

In the Restaurant

I have (We have) a reservation.	*J'ai (Nous avons) une réservation.* zhay (noo zah-vohNz) ewn ray-sehr-vah-syohN
How long will I have (we have) to wait?	*Combien de temps dois-je (devons-nous) attendre?* kohN-byaN duh tahN dwahzh (duh-vohN-noo) ah-tahNdr
Is there a cover charge?	*Il y a un couvert?* eel yah uhN koo-vehr
Where are the bathrooms?	*Où sont les toilettes?* oo sohN lay twah-leht
This has a chip.	*Ceci a une ébréchure.* suh-see ah ewn ay-bray-shoor
This is dirty.	*Ceci est sale.* suh-see eh sahl
I need …	*J'ai besoin …* zhay buh-zwaN
a bowl.	*d'un bol.* duhN bohl
a cup.	*d'une tasse.* dewn tahs
a fork.	*d'une fourchette.* dewn foor-sheht
a glass.	*d'un verre.* duhN vehr
a knife.	*d'un couteau.* duhN koo-to
a menu.	*d'un menu (d'une carte).* duhN muh-new (dewn kahrt)
a napkin.	*d'une serviette.* dewn sehr-vyeht
a place setting.	*d'un couvert.* duhN koo-vehr
a plate.	*d'une assiette.* dewn ah-syeht
a saucer.	*d'une soucoupe.* dewn soo-koop

continues

a soup bowl.	*d'un bol à soupe.* duhN bohl ah soop
a soup spoon.	*d'une cuillère à soupe.* dewn kwee-yehr ah soop
a spoon.	*d'une cuillère.* dewn kwee-yehr
a tablecloth.	*d'une nappe.* dewn nahp
a teaspoon.	*d'une petite cuillère.* dewn puh-teet kwee-yehr
a wine glass.	*d'un verre à vin.* duhN vehr ah vaN
Please bring us (me) the menu.	*Apportez-nous (-moi) le menu (la carte) s'il vous plaît.* ah-pohr-tay-nous (-mwah) luh muh-new (lah kahrt) seel voo pleh
Please bring us (me) some bread.	*Apportez-nous (-moi) du pain s'il vous plaît.* ah-pohr-tay-noo (-mwah) dew paN seel voo pleh
Do you have a menu in English?	*Avez-vous un menu (une carte) en anglais?* ah-vay-voo uhN muh-new (ewn kahrt) ahN nahN-gleh
Do you have a children's menu?	*Avez-vous un menu (une carte) enfant?* ah-vay-voo uhN muh-new (ewn kahrt) ahN-fahN
We'd (I'd) like the fixed-price menu.	*Nous voudrions (Je voudrais) le menu (la carte) à prix fixe.* noo voo-dree-yohN (zhuh voo-dreh) luh muh-new (lah kahrt) ah pree feeks
What's today's special?	*Quelle est la spécialité du jour?* kehl eh lah spay-syah-lee-tay dew zhoor
What's the house specialty?	*Quelle est la spécialité de la maison?* kehl eh lay spay-syah-lee-tay duh lah meh-zohN

| What do you recommend? | *Qu'est-ce que vous recommandez?*
 kehs-kuh voo ruh-koh-mahN-day |
| We would like (I would like) to order. | *Nous voudrions (Je voudrais) commander.*
 noo voo-dree-yohN (zhuh voo-dreh) koh-mahN-day |

Understanding the Menu

A French menu can seem confusing and overwhelming unless you know certain culinary terms. The following will help you interpret sauce names and other items on a French menu.

à la bonne femme ah lah bohn fahm	A poached dish (usually fish) prepared with a white wine sauce
aïoli ah-yoh-lee	A mayonnaise flavored with garlic
alsacienne ahl-sah-syehn	A dish with sauerkraut
béarnaise bay-ahr-nehz	A butter and egg sauce flavored with wine, shallots, and tarragon
bercy behr-see	A white sauce generally served with fish
beurre blanc buhr blahN	Butter sauce flavored with shallots and white wine
blanquette blahN-keht	A creamy egg and white wine sauce, usually served with stew
bordelaise bohr-duh-lehz	A dish prepared with Bordeaux wine
bourguignonne boor-gee-noyhn	A dish prepared with Burgundy wine

continues

bretonne breh-tohn	A dish prepared with beans
chantilly shahN-tee-yee	Whipped cream
crécy kray-see	A dish made with carrots
daube dob	A stew, usually beef, with red wine, onions, and garlic
diable dee-yahbl	A spicy sauce
duxelles dooks-ehl	A dish prepared with a mushroom mixture
farci(e) fahr-see	A dish that has stuffing
financière fee-nahN-syehr	A dish made with Madeira wine and truffles
fines herbes feen zehrb	Various herbs
florentine floh-rahN-teen	A dish made with spinach
forestière foh-rehs-tyehr	A dish made with wild mushrooms
hollandaise oh-lahN-dehz	An egg yolk and butter sauce with lemon juice or vinegar
jardinière zhahr-dee-nyehr	A dish made with vegetables
lyonnaise lee-oh-nehz	A dish made with onions
maître d'hôtel mehtr do-tehl	A butter sauce made with parsley and lemon juice
meunière muh-nyehr	A meat or fish lightly dusted with flour, sautéed, and served in a lemon and butter sauce
mornay mohr-nay	A white sauce with cheese

normande nohr-mahNd	A fish sauce
parmentier pahr-mahN-tyay	A dish made with potatoes
périgourdine pay-ree-goor-deen	A dish made with truffles
provençale proh-vahN-sahl	A vegetable garnish
ragoût rah-goo	A stew made with meat or seafood and vegetables
rémoulade ray-moo-lahd	A mayonnaise flavored with mustard
véronique vay-roh-neek	A dish served with grapes
vol-au-vent vohl-o-vahN	Creamed meat served in a puff pastry shell

Ordering a Meal

Appetizers

artichokes in vinaigrette dressing	*les artichauts à la vinaigrette* lay zahr-tee-sho ah lah vee-neh-greht
sliced raw vegetables, usually in a vinaigrette sauce	*les crudités variées* lay krew-dee-tay vah-ryay
snails cooked in butter and garlic	*les escargots à la bourguignonne* lay zehs-kahr-go ah lah boor-gee-nyohn
duck or goose liver served with slices of French bread	*le fois gras* luh fwah grah
puréed liver or other meat served in a loaf	*le pâté* luh pah-tay
fish dumplings served in a white sauce	*les quenelles* lay kuh-nehl

continues

egg custard tart prepared with meat	*la quiche lorraine* lah keesh loh-rehn
a pork mixture spread, usually served with French bread	*les rillettes* lay ree-yeht
a type of meat, game, or fish pâté served in a deep dish	*la terrine* lah teh-reen

Soups

What's the soup of the day?	*Quelle est la soupe du jour?* kehl eh lah soop dew zhoor
I'll have …	*Je prends …* zhuh prahN
the creamy soup made with crayfish.	*la bisque.* lah beesk
the seafood stew.	*la bouillabaisse.* lah boo-yah-behs
the clear broth.	*le consommé.* luh kohN-soh-may
the rich consommé served with vegetables and meat.	*la petite marmite.* lah puh-teet mahr-meet
the thick soup made of puréed vegetables.	*le potage.* luh poh-tahzh
the onion soup served with bread and cheese.	*la soupe à l'oignon.* lah soop ah loh-nyohN
the creamy chicken (tomato) soup.	*le velouté de volaille (de tomate).* luh vuh-loo-tay duh voh-lah-y (duh toh-maht)

Meats

I'd like ...	*Je voudrais ...* zhuh voo-dreh
the beef.	*le bœuf.* luh buhf
the filet mignon.	*le filet mignon.* luh fee-leh mee-nyohN
the ham.	*le jambon.* luh zhahN-bohN
a hamburger.	*un hamburger.* uhN ahN-boor-guhr
the lamb.	*l'agneau.* lah-nyo
the lamb chops.	*les côtes d'agneau.* lay kot dah-nyo
the leg of lamb.	*le gigot d'agneau.* le zhee-goh dah-nyo
the rack of lamb.	*le carré d'agneau.* luh kah-ray dah-nyo
the liver.	*le foie.* luh fwah
the meatballs.	*les boulettes de viande.* lay boo-leht duh vyahNd
the pork.	*le porc.* luh pohr
the pork chops.	*les côtes de porc.* lay kot duh pohr
the roast beef.	*le rosbif.* luh rohs-beef
the sausages.	*les saucisses.* lay so-sees
the steak.	*le bifteck.* luh beef-tehk
the stew.	*le ragoût.* luh rah-goo
the veal.	*le veau.* luh vo
the veal chops.	*les côtes de veau.* lay kot duh vo

Fowl & Game

I'd like ...	*Je voudrais ...*
	zhuh voo-dreh
the chicken (stuffed).	*le poulet (farci).*
	luh poo-leh (fahr-see)
a chicken breast.	*un blanc de poulet.*
	uhN blahN duh poo-leh
the dark meat.	*les cuisses de poulet.*
	lay kwees duh poo-leh
the chicken fingers.	*des bâtonnets de poulet pané.*
	day bah-toh-neh duh poo-leh pah-nay
the drumstick.	*le pilon.*
	luh pee-lohN
the duck.	*le canard.*
	luh kah-nahr
the goose.	*l'oie.*
	lwah
the quail.	*la caille.*
	lah kah-y
the rabbit.	*le lapin.*
	luh lah-paN
the turkey (stuffed).	*la dinde (farcie).*
	lah daNd (fahr-see)
the venison.	*la venaison.*
	lah vuh-neh-zohN

Fish & Seafood

I'll have ...	*Je prends ...*
	zhuh prahN
the anchovies.	*les anchois.*
	lay zahN-shwah
the clams.	*les palourdes.*
	lay pah-loord
the codfish.	*le cabillaud.*
	luh kah-bee-yo
the crabs.	*les crabes.*
	lay krahb

the flounder.	*le flet.* luh fleh
the grouper.	*le mérou.* luh may-roo
the halibut.	*le flétan.* luh flay-tahN
the lobster.	*le homard.* luh oh-mahr
the mackerel.	*le maquereau.* luh mah-kro
the monkfish.	*la lotte.* lah loht
the mussels.	*les moules.* lay mool
the octopus.	*le poulpe.* luh poolp
the oysters.	*les huîtres.* lay zweetr
the prawns.	*les crevettes.* lay kruh-veht
the red snapper.	*le vivaneau rouge.* luh vee-vah-no roozh
the scallops.	*les coquilles.* lay koh-kee-y
the sea bass.	*le loup de mer.* luh loo duh mehr
the shrimp.	*les crevettes.* lay kruh-veht
the snails.	*les escargots.* lay zehs-kahr-go
the sole.	*la sole.* lah sohl
the squid.	*le calamar.* luh kah-lah-mahr
the swordfish.	*l'espadon.* lehs-pah-dohN
the trout.	*la truite.* lah trweet
the tuna.	*le thon.* luh tohN

Food Preparation

If you'd like to have your meat prepared the way
you prefer it, keep in mind that French chefs have
a different interpretation of rare, medium, and well
done than most American restaurants. Rare means
barely cooked, medium is just a bit more than our
rare, and well done is a bit more than our medium.

I prefer the dish ...	*Je préfère le plat ...* zhuh pray-fehr luh plah
baked.	*cuit au four.* kwee to foor
boiled.	*bouilli.* boo-yee
breaded.	*pané.* pah-nay
broiled.	*rôti.* ro-tee
browned.	*caramelisé.* kah-rah-meh-lee-zay
chopped.	*hâché.* ah-shay
with the dressing (sauce) on the side.	*avec la sauce à côté.* ah-vehk lah sos ah ko-tay
fried.	*frit.* free
grilled.	*grillé.* gree-yay
mashed.	*écrasé.* ay-krah-zay
poached.	*poché.* poh-shay
roasted.	*rôti.* ro-tee

with a lot of (a little) sauce.	*avec beaucoup de (peu de) sauce.* ah-vehk bo-koo duh (puh duh) sos
sautéed.	*sauté.* so-tay
smoked.	*fumé.* few-may
steamed.	*à la vapeur.* ah lah vah-puhr
stewed.	*à l'étuvée.* ah lay-tew-vay
very rare.	*bleu.* bluh
rare.	*saignant.* seh-nyahN
medium rare.	*rosé.* ro-zay
medium.	*à point.* ah pwaN
medium well done.	*moyen bien cuit.* mwah-yaN byaN kwee
well done.	*bien cuit.* byaN kwee

Vegetables

When you don't want something, the definite article (*le*, *la*, *l'*, *les*) is replaced by *de* (*d'*).

I won't have any cauliflower.

Je ne prends pas de chou-fleur.
zhuh nuh prahN pah duh shoo-fluhr

We won't have any onions.

Nous ne prenons pas d'oignons.
noo nuh pruh-nohN pah doh-nyohN

I'll have …	*Je prends …* zhuh prahN
artichokes.	*les artichauts.* lay zahr-tee-sho
asparagus.	*les asperges.* lay zahs-pehrzh
beans (green).	*les haricots verts.* lay zah-ree-ko vehr
beets.	*les betteraves.* lay bay-trahv
broccoli.	*le brocoli.* luh broh-koh-lee
carrots.	*les carottes.* lay kah-roht
cauliflower.	*le chou-fleur.* luh shoo-fluhr
celery.	*le céleri.* luh sayl-ree
corn.	*le maïs.* luh mah-ees
cucumbers.	*les conconbres.* lay kohN-kohNbr
eggplant.	*l'aubergine.* lo-behr-zheen
lettuce.	*la laitue.* lah lay-tew
mushrooms.	*les champignons.* lay shahN-pee-nyohN
onions.	*les oignons.* lay zoh-nyohN
peas.	*les petits pois.* lay puh-tee pwah
potatoes.	*les pommes de terre.* lay pohm duh tehr
rice.	*le riz.* luh ree
spinach.	*les épinards.* lay zay-pee-nahr
squash.	*la courge.* lah koorzh

sweet potato.	*la patate douce.* lah pah-taht doos
tomato.	*la tomate.* lah toh-maht
zucchini.	*la courgette.* lah koo-zheht

Condiments, Herbs & Spices

The French use lots of herbs, spices, seasonings, and condiments to flavor their foods. Depend on menu descriptions or your server to help you determine whether the dish will be to your liking.

I like (I don't like) …	*J'aime (Je n'aime pas)* … zhehm (zhuh nehm pah)
basil.	*le basilic.* luh bah-see-leek
cumin.	*le cumin.* luh kew-maN
dill.	*l'aneth.* ah-neht
garlic.	*l'ail.* lah-y
ginger.	*le gingembre.* luh zhaN-zhaNbr
honey.	*le miel.* luh myehl
horseradish.	*le raifort.* luh reh-fohr
ketchup.	*le ketchup.* luh keht-shuhp
mayonnaise.	*la mayonnaise.* lah mah-yoh-nehz
mustard.	*la moutarde.* lah moo-tahrd
oil.	*l'huile.* lweel

continues

oregano.	*l'origan.* loh-ree-gahN
paprika.	*le paprika.* luh pah-pree-kah
parsley.	*le persil.* luh pehr-seel
pepper.	*le poivre.* luh pwahvr
rosemary.	*le romarin.* luh roh-mah-rahN
salt.	*le sel.* luh sehl
sesame.	*le sésame.* luh say-zahm
sugar.	*le sucre.* luh sewkr
tarragon.	*l'estragon.* ehs-trah-gohN
thyme.	*le thym.* luh taN
vinegar.	*le vinaigre.* luh vee-nehgr

Special Requests

I'm on a diet.	*Je suis au régime.* zhuh zwee zo ray-zheem
I'm vegan.	*Je suis végétalien(ne).* zhuh swee vay-zhay-tah-lyaN (-lyehn)
I'm a vegetarian.	*Je suis végétarien(ne).* zhuh swee vay-zhay-tah-ryaN (-ryehn)
I have food allergies (sensitivities).	*J'ai des allergies (sensibilités) alimentaires.* zhay day zah-lehr-zhee (sahN-see-bee-lee-tay) ah-lee-mahN-tehr
What are the ingredients?	*Quels sont les ingrédients?* kehl sohN lay zaN-gray-dyahN

Please ask the chef.	*Demandez au chef* *s'il vous plaît.* duh-mahN-day o shehf seel voo pleh
I can't have any …	*Je ne tolère pas …* zhuh nuh toh-lehr pah
alcohol.	*l'alcool.* lahl-kohl
dairy products.	*les produits laitiers.* lay proh-dwee leh-tyay
eggs.	*les œufs.* lay zuh
fish.	*le poisson.* luh pwah-sohN
gluten.	*le gluten.* luh glew-tehn
milk.	*le lait.* luh leh
peanuts.	*les cacahuètes.* lay kah-kah-weht
saturated fats.	*les graisses saturées.* lay grahs sah-tew-ray
shellfish.	*les crustacés.* lay krew-stah-say
soy.	*le soja.* luh soh-zhah
wheat.	*le blé.* luh blay
I'm looking for a dish that is …	*Je cherche un plat … .* zhuh shehrsh uhN plah
fat-free	*sans gras.* sahN grah
gluten-free	*sans gluten.* sahN glew-tehn
high in fiber.	*riche en fibre.* reesh ahN feebr
low in cholesterol.	*faible en cholestérol.* fehbl ahN koh-lehs-tay-rohl
low in fat.	*faible en gras.* fehbl ahN grah

continues

low in sodium.	*faible en sodium.* fehbl ahN soh-dyuhm
non-dairy	*non-laitier* nohN leh-tyay
non-spicy	*non-épicé* nohN nay-pee-say
organic	*biologique* byoh-loh-zheek
salt-free(.)	*sans sel(.)* sahN sehl
sugar-free(.)	*sans sucre(.)* sahN sewkr
without artificial coloring.	*sans colorants artificiels.* sahN koh-loh-rahN ahr-tee-fee-syehl
without butter (cheese) (cream) (garlic) (onions).	*sans beurre (fromage)* *(crème) (ail) (oignons).* sahN buhr (froh-mahzh) (krehm) (ah-y) (oh-nyohN)
without preservatives.	*sans conservateurs.* sahN kohn-sehr-vah-tuhr

Beverages

In France, *un apéritif* (uhN nah-pay-ree-teef) is an
appetite stimulant. Among the most popular are
Suze, Lillet, Byrrh, Dubonnet, kir, pastis, vermouth,
and Chartreuse.

The French usually drink wine with dinner. If
you're particular about your wine, ask to speak
to the wine specialist, *le sommelier/la sommelière*
(luh soh-meh-lyay/lah soh-meh-lyehr).

Un digestif (uhN dee-zhehs-teef) is an alcoholic
drink served at the end of the meal. Among
the more popular are armagnac, Bénédictine,
Chambord, cognac, Cointreau, crème de cassis,
crème de menthe, and Grand Marnier.

I'm thirsty.	*J'ai soif.* zhay swahf
I'd like to speak to the wine specialist.	*Je voudrais parler au sommelier (à la sommelière).* zhuh voo-dreh pahr-lay o soh-meh-lyay (ah lah soh-meh-lyehr)
I'd like …	*Je voudrais …* zhuh voo-dreh
a (light, dark, draft, craft) beer.	*une bière (légère, brune, à la pression, artisanale).* zewn byehr (lay-zhehr, brewn, ah lah preh-syohN, ahr-tee-zah-nahl)
champagne.	*du champagne.* dew shahN-pah-nyuh
coffee (decaffeinated) (iced) (black) … .	*du café (décaféiné) (glacé) (noir) … .* dew kah-fay (day-kah-fay- ee-nay) (glah-say) (nwahr)
with cream (milk) (sugar)	*avec café-crème (au lait) (sucré).* ah-vehk kah-fay-krehm (o leh) (sew-kray)
an espresso.	*un expresso.* uhN nehks-preh-so
a lemonade.	*un citronnade.* uhN see-troh-nahd
milk.	*du lait.* dew leh
mineral water (sparkling) (flat).	*de l'eau minérale (gazeuse) (plate).* duh lo mee-nay-rahl (gah-zuhz) (plaht)
soda (diet).	*un soda light.* uhN soh-dah light
tea (iced) … .	*un thé (glacé) … .* uhN tay glah-say
with lemon (milk) (sugar)	*au citron (au lait) (sucré).* o see-trohN (au leh) (sew-kray)

continues

water.	*de l'eau.* duh lo
a glass of … wine.	*un verre de vin …* uhN vehr duh vaN
red	*rouge.* roozh
rosé	*rosé.* ro-zay
white	*blanc.* blahN
dry	*sec.* sehk
sweet	*doux.* doo
sparkling	*mousseux.* moo-suh
a glass (a bottle) of champagne.	*un verre (une bouteille) de champagne.* uhN vehr (ewn boo-teh-y) duh shahN-pah-nyuh
Is the water filtered?	*Est-ce que l'eau est filtrée?* ehs-kuh lo eh feel-tray

Note that in many places, if you order *un café*, you'll get espresso, not regular brewed coffee.

Salads

In France, it's traditional to have *une salade* (ewn sah-lahd) followed by *des fromages variés* (day froh-mahzh vah-ryay) at the end of the meal, after the meat course, and before dessert.

Please bring me a green (mixed) salad.	*Apportez-moi une salade verte s'il vous plait.* ah-pohr-tay-mwah ewn sah-lahd vehrt seel-voo-pleh
Please put the salad dressing on the side.	*Mettez la vinaigrette (la sauce) à côté s'il vous plaît.* meh-tay lah vee-neh-greht (lah sos) ah ko-tay seel voo pleh
Please don't put any dressing on my salad.	*Ne mettez pas de vinaigrette (de sauce) sur ma salade s'il vous plaît.* nuh meh-tay pah duh vee-neh-greht (de sos) sewr mah sah-lahd seel voo pleh

Cheeses

Popular cheeses include boursin, brie, camembert, chèvre, gruyère, munster, port-salut, and roquefort.

What's that cheese?	*Quel est ce fromage?* kehl eh suh froh-mahzh
Is it ... ?	*Est-il ... ?* eh-teel
mild	*doux* doo
sharp	*piquant* pee-kahN
hard	*à pâte dure* ah paht dewr
soft	*à pâte molle* ah paht mohl

Desserts

I'd like ...	*Je voudrais ...* zhuh voo-dreh
a slice of (chocolate) cake.	*une tranche de gâteau (au chocolat).* ewn trahNsh duh gah-to (o shoh-koh-lah)
caramel custard.	*de la crème caramel.* duh lah krehm kah-rah-mehl
cookies.	*des biscuits.* day bees-kwee
ice cream.	*une glace (une bombe).* ewn glahs (ewn bohNb)
a bowl of ... ice cream.	*un bol de glace ... .* uhN bohl duh glahs
a ... ice cream cone.	*un cornet de glace ... .* uhN kohr-neh duh glahs
vanilla	*à la vanille* ah lah vah-nee-y
chocolate	*au chocolat* o shoh-koh-lah
strawberry	*aux fraises* o frehz
pistachio	*aux pistaches* o pees-tahsh
a slice of (apple) pie.	*une part de tarte (aux pommes).* ewn pahr duh tahrt (o pohm)
sorbet.	*un sorbet.* uhN sohr-beh
a/an (apple) tart.	*une tarte (aux pommes).* ewn tahrt (o pohm)
Bavarian cream.	*un bavarois.* uhN bah-vahr-wah
doughnuts.	*des beignets.* day beh-nyeh
a waffle.	*une gaufre.* ewn gofr

meringues in custard sauce.	*des œufs à la neige.* day zuh ah lah nehzh
baked Alaska.	*une omelette norvégienne.* ewn ohm-leht nohr-vay-zhyehn
poached pears Belle Helene.	*des poires Belle-Hélène.* day pwahr behl-ay-lehn
cream puffs with ice cream and chocolate sauce.	*des profiteroles.* day proh-fee-trohl
sponge cake with pudding.	*une charlotte.* ewn shahr-loht
(chocolate) mousse.	*une mousse (au chocolat).* ewn moos (o shoh-koh-lah)
fruit salad.	*une macédoine de fruits.* ewn mah-say-dwahn duh frwee
soufflé.	*un soufflé.* uhN soo-flay
yogurt.	*un yaourt.* uhN yah-oort

Fruits

apple	*la pomme* lah pohm
apricot	*l'abricot* (m.) lah-bree-ko
banana	*la banane* lah bah-nahn
blackberry	*la mûre* lah mewr
blueberry	*la myrtille* lah meer-tee-y
cherry	*la cerise* lah suh-reez
coconut	*la noix de coco* lah nwah duh koh-ko
grape	*le raisin* luh reh-zaN

continues

grapefruit	*le pamplemousse*
	luh pahN-pluh-moos
lemon	*le citron*
	luh see-trohN
lime	*le citron vert*
	luh see-trohN vehr
melon	*le melon*
	luh muh-lohN
orange	*l'orange* (f.)
	loh-rahNzh
peach	*la pêche*
	lah pehsh
pear	*la poire*
	lah pwahr
pineapple	*l'ananas* (m.)
	lah-nah-nah
plum	*la prune*
	lah prewn
prune	*le pruneau*
	luh prew-no
raisin	*le raisin sec*
	luh reh-zaN sehk
raspberry	*la framboise*
	lah frahN-bwahz
strawberry	*la fraise*
	lah frehz
watermelon	*la pastèque*
	lah pahs-tehk

Paying the Tab

The bill please.	*L'addition s'il vous plaît.*
	lah-dee-syohN seel voo pleh
Separate checks please.	*Des additions séparées*
	s'il vous plaît.
	day zah-dee-syohN say-pah-ray
	seel voo pleh
Is the tip (service) included?	*Le service est compris?*
	luh sehr-vees eh kohN-pree

I think there's a mistake.	*Je crois qu'il y a une erreur.* zhuh krwah keel yah ewn eh-ruhr
This wasn't ordered.	*On n'a pas commandé ceci.* ohN nah pah koh-mahN-day suh-see
Thank you. Everything was delicious.	*Merci. Tout était délicieux.* mehr-see too tay-teh day-lee-syuh

Specialty Shops

bakery	*la boulangerie* lah boo-lahNzh-ree
butcher shop	*la boucherie* lah boosh-ree
candy store	*la confiserie* lah kohN-fee-zree
dairy store	*la crémerie* lah kray-mree
fish store	*la poissonnerie* lah pwah-sohn-ree
fruit store	*la fruiterie* lah frwee-tree
grocery (vegetable) store	*l'épicerie* (f.) lay-pee-sree
liquor store	*le magasin de vins* *et spiritueux* luh mah-gah-zaN duh vaN ay spee-ree-tew-uh
market	*le marché* luh mahr-shay
pastry shop	*la pâtisserie* lah pah-tee-sree
supermarket (very big supermarket)	*le supermarché* *(l'hypermarché)* luh soo-pehr-mahr-shay (lee-pehr-mahr-shay

Quantities

In French-speaking countries, the metric system is used when measuring quantities of food. Liquids are measured in liters and solids are measured in grams and kilograms. Use the following expressions if you go shopping.

I need ...	*J'ai besoin ...* zhay buh-zwaN
a bag of (flour).	*d'un sac de (farine).* duhN sahk duh (fah-reen)
a bar of (chocolate).	*d'une tablette de (chocolat).* dewn tah-bleht duh (shoh-koh-lah)
a bottle of (water).	*d'une bouteille de (d'eau minérale).* dewn boo-teh-y duh (do mee-nay-rahl)
a box of (cereal).	*d'une boîte de (céréales).* dewn bwaht duh (say-ray-ahl)
a can of (soup).	*d'une boîte de (soupe).* dewn bwaht duh (soop)
a dozen (eggs).	*d'une douzaine (d'œufs).* dewn doo-zehn (duh)
a jar of (coffee).	*d'un pot de (café).* duhN po duh (kah-fay)
a liter of (milk).	*d'un litre de (lait).* duhN leetr duh (leh)
a package of (cheese).	*d'un paquet de (fromage).* duhN pah-keh duh (froh-mahzh)
6 slices of (ham).	*de six tranches de (jambon).* de see trahNsh duh (zhahN-bohN)

100 grams of (butter). [about ¼ pound]	*de cent grammes de (beurre).* duh sahN grahm duh (buhr)
200 grams of (oranges). [about ½ pound]	*de deux cents grammes (d'oranges).* duh duh sahN grahm (doh-rahNzh)
½ kilogram of (grapes). [about 1 pound]	*de cinq cents grammes de (raisins).* duh saNk sahN grahm duh (reh-zaN)
1 kilogram of (turkey). [about 2 pounds]	*d'un kilo de (dinde).* duhN kee-lo duh (daNd)
2½ kilograms of (potatoes). [about 5 pounds]	*deux kilos et demi de (pommes de terre).* duh duh kee-lo ay duh-mee duh (pohm duh tehr)
Add …	*Ajoutez …* ah-zhoo-tay
a little (salt).	*un peu de (sel).* uhN puh duh (sehl)
a lot of (pepper).	*beaucoup de (poivre).* bo-koo duh (pwahvr)
enough (sugar).	*assez de (sucre).* ah-say duh (sewkr)

Use *trop de* (tro duh) to express "too much."

There's too much garlic in the stew.

Il y a trop d'ail dans le ragoût.
eel yah tro dah-y dahN luh rah-goo

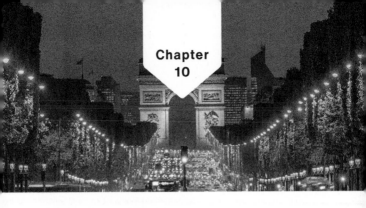

Shopping

The souvenirs you pick up while traveling will remind you and your loved ones of your trip for years to come. You'll undoubtedly want to select perfect gifts and mementos—whether you opt for clothing or regional handicrafts. No matter what your preference, this chapter will help you purchase those special items.

The sales tax on goods and services in France is known as TVA (*taxe sur la valeur ajoutée* [tahks sewr lah vah-luhr ah-zhoo-tay; value-added tax [VAT]). Different tax rates are applied on different categories of goods and services. Keep receipts for all your purchases because you might be eligible for a refund on the taxes you've paid. Specially marked kiosks in the airport or at large department stores will help you determine whether money is owed to you.

Stores

The following are some stores (*les magasins* [lay mah-gah-zaN]) that might interest you.

I'm looking for … .	*Je cherche … .* zhuh shehrsh
Where's … ?	*Où se trouve … ?* oo suh troov
a bookstore	*une librairie* ewn lee-breh-ree
a clothing store …	*un magasin* *de vêtements …* uhN mah-gah-zaN duh veht-mahN
for women	*pour femmes* poor fahm
for men	*pour hommes* poor ohm
for children	*pour enfants* poor ahN-fahN
a department store	*un grand magasin* uhN grahN mah-gah-zaN
a florist	*un fleuriste* uhN fluh-reest
a jewelry store	*une bijouterie* ewn bee-zhoo-tree
a liquor store	*un magasin de vins* *et spiritueux* uhN mah-gah-zaN duh vaN ay spee-ree-tew-uh
a mall	*un centre commercial* uhN sahNtr koh-mehr-syahl
a market	*un marché* uhN mahr-shay
a newsstand	*un kiosk à journaux* uhN kee-ohsk ah zhoor-no
a shoe store	*un magasin de chaussures* uhN mah-gah-zaN duh sho-sewr

a souvenir shop	*un magasin de souvenirs*
	uhN mah-gah-zaN duh
	soov-neer

| a tobacco store | *un bureau de tabac* |
| | uhN bew-ro duh tah-bah |

a toy store	*un magasin de jouets*
	uhN mah-gah-zaN duh
	zhoo-eh

General Questions

| Where can I find ... ? | *Où puis-je trouver ... ?* |
| | oo pweezh troo-vay |

Could you please help me?	*Pourriez-vous m'aider*
	s'il vous plaît?
	poo-ryay-voo may-day
	seel voo pleh

| Do you sell ... ? | *Vendez-vous ... ?* |
| | vahN-day voo |

Could you please show me ... ?	*Pourriez-vous me montrer ... s'il vous plait?*
	poo-ryay-voo muh mohN-tray
	... seel voo pleh

| Where is (are) ... ? | *Où est (sont) ... ?* |
| | oo eh (sohN) |

| How much does it cost? | *Ça coûte combien?* |
| | sah koot kohN-byaN |

| What's the price? | *Quel est le prix?* |
| | kehl eh luh pree |

| Are there any sales? | *Il y a des soldes?* |
| | eel yah day sohld |

Is there a discount?	*Il y a une remise (un rabais)?*
	eel yah ewn ruh-meez
	(uhN rah-beh)

| How much is it? | *C'est combien?* |
| | seh kohN-byaN |

| Where do I pay? | *Où dois-je payer?* |
| | oo dwahzh pay-yay |

continues

Could you put it (them) in a bag (a box)?	*Pourriez-vous le/la (les) mettre dans un sac (une boîte)?* poo-ryay-voo luh/lah (lay) mehtr dahN zuhN sahk s(zewn bwaht)
Do you accept credit (debit) cards?	*Acceptez-vous les cartes de crédit (débit)?* ahks-ehp-tay-voo lay kahrt duh kray-dee (day-bee)
Which ones do you accept?	*Lesquelles acceptez-vous?* lay-kehl ahks-ehp-tay-voo
My card has (doesn't have) a chip.	*Ma carte a une (n'a pas de) puce.* mah kahrt ah ewn (nah pah duh) pews
Where should I insert it?	*Où dois-je l'insérer?* oo dwahzh laN-say-ray
Where do I sign?	*Où dois-je signer?* oo dwahzh see-nyay
Can I return my purchase?	*Puis-je rapporter mon achat?* pweezh rah-pohr-tay mohN nah-shah
Could you give me a receipt?	*Pourriez-vous me donner un reçu?* poo-ryay-voo muh doh-nay uhN ruh-sew
Could you gift wrap this?	*Pourriez-vous emballer ceci en cadeau?* poo-ryay-voo ahN-bah-lay suh-see ahN kah-do
Could you send this to the United States?	*Pourriez-vous envoyer ceci aux États-Unis?* poo-ryay-voo zahN-vwah-yay suh-see o zay-tah-zew-nee

General Statements

I'm just looking.	*Je regarde tout simplement.* zhuh ruh-gahrd too sahNpl-mahN
I'm looking for … .	*Je cherche … .* zhuh shehrsh
I want (don't want) to spend a lot.	*Je veux (ne veux pas) dépenser beaucoup.* zhuh vuh (nuh vuh pah) day-pahN-say bo-koo
I can't find what I'm looking for.	*Je ne peux pas trouver ce que je cherche.* zhuh nuh puh pah troo-vay suh kuh zhuh shehrsh
Show me where it is please.	*Montrez-moi où le (la) trouver s'il vous plaît.* mohN-tray-mwah oo luh (lah) troo-vay seel voo pleh
I'd like to return this.	*Je voudrais rapporter ceci.* zhuh voo-dreh rah-pohr-tay suh-see
It doesn't work.	*Il (Elle) ne marche pas.* eel (ehl) nuh mahrsh pah
It doesn't fit me.	*Il (Elle) ne me va pas bien.* eel (ehl) nuh muh vah pah byaN
I'd like to exchange this.	*Je voudrais échanger ceci.* zhuh voo-dreh ay-sahN-zhay suh-see
I'd like a refund please.	*Je voudrais un remboursement s'il vous plaît.* zhuh voo-dreh uhN rahN-boors-mahN seel voo pleh
I don't want store credit.	*Je ne voudrais pas de crédit de magasin.* zhuh nuh voo-dreh pah duh kray-dee duh mah-gah-zaN

Bookstore or Newsstand

Do you sell … (in English)?	*Vendez-vous des … (en anglais)?* vahN-day-voo day … (ahN nahN-gleh)
books (for children)	*livres (enfantins)* leevr (ahN-fahN-taN)
guides	*guides* geed
magazines	*revues* ruh-vew
maps (city street maps)	*cartes (plans de la ville)* kahrt (plahN duh lah veel)
newspapers	*journaux* zhoor-no
I'd like to buy a bilingual (French–English) pocket dictionary.	*Je voudrais acheter un dictionnaire de poche bilingue (français–anglais).* zhuh voo-dreh ahsh-tay uhN deek-syoh-nehr duh pohsh bee-laNg (frahN-seh–ahN-gleh)

Clothing Store

Clothing Items

I'm looking for …	*Je cherche …* zhuh shehrsh
a bathing suit.	*un maillot de bain.* uhN mah-yo duh baN
a belt.	*une ceinture.* ewn saN-tewr
a blazer.	*un blazer.* uhN blah-zehr
a blouse.	*un chemisier.* uhN shuh-mee-zyay
boots.	*des bottes.* day boht

boxer shorts.	*un boxer.* uhN bohks-ehr
a bra.	*un soutien-gorge.* uhN soo-tyaN-gohrzh
briefs.	*un slip.* uhN sleep
a cap.	*une casquette.* ewn kahs-keht
capris (cropped pants).	*un pantacourt.* uhN pahn-tah-koor
a dress.	*une robe.* ewn rohb
gloves.	*des gants.* (m.) day gahN
a hat.	*un chapeau.* uhN shah-po
a hoodie.	*un sweat à capuche.* uhN sweht ah kah-pewsh
a jacket.	*une veste.* ewn vehst
jeans.	*un jean.* uhN dzheen
an overcoat.	*un manteau.* uhN mahN-to
pajamas.	*un pyjama.* uhN pee-zhah-mah
(a pair of) panties.	*une culotte.* ewn kew-loht
pants.	*un pantalon.* uhN pahn-tah-lohN
pantyhose.	*des collants.* (m.) day koh-lahN
a pocketbook.	*un sac.* uhN sahk
a raincoat.	*un imperméable.* uhN naN-pehr-may-ahbl
a robe.	*une robe de chambre.* ewn rohb duh shahNbr
sandals.	*des sandales.* (f.) day sahN-dahl

continues

a scarf.	*une écharpe.* ewn ay-shahrp
a shirt.	*une chemise.* ewn shuh-meez
shoes.	*des chaussures.* (f.) / *des souliers.* (m.) day sho-sewr / day soo-lyay
shorts.	*un short.* uhN shohrt
a skirt.	*une jupe.* ewn zhoop
slippers.	*des pantoufles.* (f.) day pahN-toofl
sneakers.	*des baskets.* (f.) / *des tennis.* (m.) day bahs-keht / day tay-nees
socks.	*des chaussettes.* (f.) day sho-seht
a sports coat.	*une veste sport.* ewn vehst spohr
stockings.	*des bas.* (m.) day bah
a suit (man's).	*un costume (un complet).* uhN kohs-tewm (uhN kohN-pleh)
a suit (woman's).	*un tailleur.* uhN tah-yuhr
sweatpants.	*un pantalon de jogging.* uhN pahN-tah-lohN duh zhoh-geeng
a sweatshirt.	*un sweat.* uhN sweht
a sweater.	*un pull (un chandail).* uhN pewl (uhN shahN-dah-y)
a T-shirt.	*un tee-shirt.* uhN tee-shuhrt
a tie.	*une cravate.* ewn krah-vaht
an umbrella.	*un parapluie.* uhN pah-rah-plwee

an undershirt.	*un maillot de corps.* uhN mah-yo duh kohr
underwear.	*des sous-vêtements.* (m.) day soo-veht-mahN
I'd like this ...	*Je voudrais ceci ...* zhuh voo-dreh suh-see
with long sleeves.	*avec manches longues.* ah-vehk mahNsh lohNg
with short sleeves.	*avec manches courtes.* ah-vehk mahNsh koort
sleeveless.	*sans manches.* sahN mahNsh
I wear size small (medium) (large).	*Je porte une taille petite (moyenne) (grande).* zhuh pohrt ewn tah-y puh-teet (mwah-yehn) (grahNd)

Colors

Do you have this in ... ?	*Avez-vous ceci en ... ?* ah-vay-voo suh-see ahN
beige	*beige* behzh
black	*noir* nwahr
blue	*bleu* bluh
brown	*brun (marron)* bruhN (mah-rohN)
gray	*gris* gree
green	*vert* vehr
navy blue	*bleu marine* bluh mah-reen
orange	*orange* oh-rahNzh
pink	*rose* roz
purple	*pourpre* poor-pr

continues

red	*rouge*
	roozh
white	*blanc*
	blahN
yellow	*jaune*
	zhon
Do you have other colors (styles)?	*Avez-vous d'autres couleurs (styles)?*
	ah-vay-voo dotr koo-luhr (steel)
I prefer ...	*Je préfère ...*
	zhuh pray-fehr
light green.	*vert clair.*
	vehr klehr
dark blue.	*bleu foncé.*
	bluh fohN-say

Materials

When you want to ask for an article of clothing made from a specific material, use *de* to express that the item is made from that material.

I'd like to buy a cashmere sweater.

Je voudrais acheter un pull en cachemire.
zhuh voo-dreh ahsh-tay uhN pewl ahN kahsh-meer

I'd like to buy a permanent press shirt.

Je voudrais acheter une chemise de pressage permanent.
zhuh voo-dreh ahsh-tay ewn shuh-meez duh preh-sahzh pehr-mah-nahN

cashmere	*cachemire* (m.)
	kahsh-meer
chiffon	*mousseline de soie* (f.)
	moos-leen duh swah
cotton	*coton* (m.)
	koh-tohN

denim	*jean* (m.) dzheen
flannel	*flanelle* (f.) flah-nehl
lace	*dentelle* (f.) dahN-tehl
leather	*cuir* (m.) kweer
linen	*lin* (m.) laN
nylon	*nylon* (m.) nee-lohN
permanent press	*pressage permanent* (m.) preh-sahzh pehr-mah-nahN
satin	*satin* (m.) sah-taN
silk	*soie* (f.) swah
suede	*daim* (m.) daN
wool	*laine* (f.) lehn

Designs

I prefer this shirt …	*Je préfère cette chemise …* zhuh pray-fehr seht shuh-meez
in a solid color.	*dans une couleur unie.* dahN zewn koo-luhr ew-nee
with pinstripes.	*à rayures fines.* ah rah-yuhr feen
with stripes.	*à rayures.* ah rah-yuhr
with polka dots.	*à pois.* ah pwah
in plaid.	*au motif écossais.* o moh-teef ay-koh-seh
Can I try this on?	*Puis-je l'essayer?* pweezh lay-say-yay

continues

Where are the dressing rooms?	*Où sont les cabines d'essayage?* oo sohN lay kah-been day-seh-yahzh

Choices

Do you have something … ?	*Avez-vous quelque chose … ?* ah-vay-voo kehl-kuh shoz
else	*d'autre* dotr
larger	*de plus grand* duh plew grahN
smaller	*de plus petit* duh plew puh-tee
longer	*de plus long* duh plew lohN
shorter	*de plus court* duh plew koor
less expensive	*de moins cher* duh mwaN shehr
more expensive	*de plus cher* duh plew shehr
better quality	*de meilleur qualité* duh meh-yuhr kah-lee-tay
Does it come in another color?	*Ça vient dans une autre couleur?* sah vyaN dahN zewn otr koo-luhr
Does this fit me?	*Ça me va?* sah muh vah
It fits me. (It doesn't fit me.)	*Ça me va. (Ça ne me va pas).* sah muh vah (sah nuh muh vah pah)
Can you alter this?	*Pouvez-vous retoucher ceci?* poo-vay-voo ruh-too-shay suh-see
When will this be ready?	*Quand est-ce que ceci sera prêt?* kahN ehs-kuh suh-see suh-rah preh

The zipper doesn't work.	*La fermeture éclair ne marche pas.* lah fehr-muh-tewr ay-klehr nuh mahrsh pah
It's missing a button.	*Un bouton manque.* uhN boo-tohN mahNk
I like it. (I like them.)	*Je l'aime. (Je les aime.)* zhuh lehm (zhuh lay zehm)
I'll take this.	*Je prends ceci.* zhuh prahN suh-see

Shoes

Please show me that pair of shoes (boots).	*Montrez-moi cette paire de chaussures (bottes) s'il vous plaît.* mohN-tray-mwah seht pehr duh sho-sewr (boht) seel voo pleh
… the ones with the high (medium) (spiked) (wedged) heels.	*… celles à talons (hauts) (moyens) (à talons aiguilles) (à talons compensés).* … sehl ah tah-lohN (o) (mwah-yaN) (ah tah-lohN zay-gwee-y) (ah tah-lohN kohN-pahN-say)
I'd like to see those sneakers.	*Je voudrais voir ces tennis (ces baskets).* zhuh voo-dreh vwahr say tay-nees (say bahs-keht)
I wear size … .	*Je chausse du … .* zhuh shos dew
Do you have them in another color?	*Vous les avez dans une autre couleur?* voo lay zah-vay dahN zewn otr koo-luhr
They're too big (small).	*Elles sont trop grandes (petites).* ehl sohN tro grahNd (puh-teet)
They're too wide (narrow).	*Elles sont trop larges (étroites).* ehl sohN tro lahrzh (ay-trwaht)

continues

They fit me well.	*Elles me vont bien.* ehl muh vohN byaN
I'll take them.	*Je les prends.* zhuh lay prahN

Jewelry Store

I'm looking for ...	*Je cherche ...* zhuh shehrsh
a bracelet.	*un bracelet.* uhN brahs-leh
a chain.	*une chaînette.* ewn sheh-neht
a charm.	*une breloque.* ewn bruh-lohk
earrings.	*des boucles d'oreille.* day bookl doh-reh-y
a necklace.	*un collier.* uhN koh-lyay
a pin.	*une broche.* ewn brohsh
a ring.	*une bague.* ewn bahg
a watch.	*une montre.* ewn mohNtr
Is this (solid) gold?	*Est-ce en or (massif)?* ehs ahN nohr (mah-seef)
Is this gold-plated?	*Est-ce en plaqué or?* ehs ahN plah-kay ohr
Is this silver or silver-plated?	*Est-ce en argent ou en plaqué argent?* ehs ahN nahr-zhahN oo ahN plah-kay ahr-zhahN
What's that stone?	*Quel est ce bijou?* kehl eh suh bee-zhoo
I'm looking for ...	*Je cherche ...* zhuh shehrsh
an amethyst.	*une améthyste.* ewn ah-may-teest

an aquamarine.	*une aigue-marine.* ewn ehg-mah-reen
a diamond.	*un diamant.* uhN dee-yah-mahN
an emerald.	*une émeraude.* ewn aym-rod
jade.	*du jade.* dew zhahd
an onyx.	*un onyx.* uhN noh-neeks
pearls.	*des perles.* day pehrl
a ruby.	*un rubis.* uhN rew-bee
a sapphire.	*un saphir.* uhN sah-feer
a topaz.	*une topaze.* ewn toh-pahz
turquoise.	*une turquoise.* ewn tewr-kwahz

Tobacco Store

Go to a *bureau de tabac* if you have smoking needs.

I'd like to buy …	*Je voudrais acheter …* zhuh voo-dreh ahsh-tay
a package (carton) of … cigarettes.	*un paquet (une cartouche) de cigarettes de … .* uhN pah-keh (ewn kahr-toosh) duh see-gah-reht duh
an electronic cigarette (vape pen).	*une cigarette électronique.* ewn see-gah-reht ay-lehk-troh-neek
(chewing) tobacco.	*du tabac (à chiquer).* dew tah-bah (ah shee-kay)
a box of cigars.	*une boîte de cigares.* ewn bwaht duh see-gahr

continues

a cigar case.	*une boîte à cigares.* ewn bwaht ah see-gahr
a lighter.	*un briquet.* uhN bree-keh
an ashtray.	*un cendrier.* uhN sahN-dree-yay
a pipe.	*une pipe.* ewn peep
a hookah.	*une narguilé.* ewn nah-gee-lay

Liquor Store

I'd like to buy a bottle of …	*Je voudrais acheter* *une bouteille de …* zhuh voo-dreh ahsh-tay ewn boo-teh-y duh
bourbon.	*bourbon.* bewr-bohN
brandy.	*cognac.* koh-nyahk
champagne.	*champagne.* shahN-pah-nyuh
gin.	*gin.* dzheen
(red) (white) (rosé) wine.	*(rouge) (blanc) (rosé) vin.* (roozh) (blahN) (ro-zay) vaN
rum.	*rhum.* rhuhm
rye.	*rye.* rah-y
scotch.	*scotch.* skohtch
vodka.	*vodka.* vohd-kah
whiskey.	*whiskey.* wees-kee

Is it dry (fruity)?	*Est-ce sec (fruité)?* ehs sehk (frwee-tay)
Do you sell bottle openers (corkscrews)?	*Vendez-vous des décapsuleurs (des tire-bouchons)?* vahN-day-voo day day-kahp-sew-luhr (day teer-boo-shohN)

Gifts & Souvenirs

Where can I buy typical gifts (souvenirs)?	*Où puis-je acheter des cadeaux (souvenirs) typiques?* oo pweez-jh ahsh-tay day kah-do (soov-neer) tee-peek
I'd like to buy a gift for my … .	*Je voudrais acheter un cadeau à mon (ma, mes) … .* zhuh voo-dreh ahsh-tay uhN kah-do ah mohN (mah, may)
I want to spend about … dollars (euros).	*Je voudrais dépenser environ … dollars (euros).* zhuh voo-dreh day-pahN-say ahN-vee-rohN … doh-lahr (uh-ro)
I don't want to spend more than … dollars (euros).	*Je ne voudrais pas dépenser plus de … dollars (euros).* zhuh nuh voo-dreh pah day-pahN-say plew duh … doh-lahr (uh-ro)
What do you recommend?	*Qu'est-ce que vous me conseillez?* kehs-kuh voo muh kohN-say-yay
Please show me …	*Montrez-moi … s'il vous plaît.* mohN-tray-mwah … seel voo pleh
art pieces.	*les objets d'art* lay zohb-zheh dahr
crystal.	*les articles en cristal* lay zahr-teekl ahN krees-tahl
lace.	*les articles en dentelle* lay zahr-teekl ahN dahN-tehl

continues

leather goods.	*les articles de cuir* lay zahr-teekl duh kweer
perfumes.	*les parfums* lay pahr-fuhN
posters.	*les affiches* lay zah-feesh
toys.	*les jouets* lay zhweh
T-shirts.	*les tee-shirts* lay tee-shuhrt

Bargaining

How much is this?	*C'est combien?* seh kohN-byan
That's too expensive.	*C'est trop cher.* seh tro shehr
Can you lower the price?	*Pourriez-vous baisser le prix?* poo-ryay-voo bay-say luh pree
I'll give you … .	*Je vous donne … .* zhuh voo dohn
Will you accept … ?	*Accepterez-vous … ?* ahks-ehp-tray-voo
That's good.	*C'est bon.* seh bohN
We have a deal.	*Nous sommes d'accord.* noo suhm dah-kohr
It's a bargain.	*C'est une bonne affaire.* seh tewn bohn ah-fehr

Sightseeing
& Entertainment

Do you want to plan your own itinerary of things to do or take a tour? Are you heading to the ocean to participate in water sports, up to the mountains for skiing or hiking, onto the links for a round of golf, or onto the courts for a brisk tennis match? Are you a film buff or a theatergoer or do you enjoy a lively opera or an elegant ballet? Perhaps you'll spend some time with a one-armed bandit in a luxurious casino? This chapter will help you do all that and more.

Getting Information

Where's a tourist office?	*Où se trouve un office de tourisme (un syndicat d'initiative)?* oo suh troov uhN noh-fees duh too-rees-muh (uhN saN-dee-kah dee-nee-syah-teev)
What's there to see?	*Qu'est-ce qu'il y a à voir?* kehs-keel yah ah vwahr
What are the main attractions?	*Quels sont les points d'intérêt?* kehl sohN lay pwaN daN-tay-reh
Where can I buy a map (a guidebook)?	*Où puis-je acheter une carte (un guide)?* oo pweezh ahsh-tay ewn kahrt (uhN geed)
What do you recommend we see (I see)?	*Que recommandez-vous que nous voyions (je voie)?* kuh ruh-koh-mahN-day-voo kuh noo vwah-ee-yohN (zhuh vwah)
I'm looking for a guide who speaks English.	*Je cherche un(e) guide qui parle anglais.* zhuh shehrsh uhN (ewn) geed kee pahrl ahN-gleh
How much do they charge … ?	*Combien me faut-il payer … ?* kohN-byaN muh fo-teel pay-yay
by the hour	*de l'heure* duh luhr
by the day	*de la journée* duh lah zhoor-nay
per person	*par personne* pahr pehr-sohn

Attractions

We would like (I would like) to see …	*Nous voudrions (Je voudrais) voir …* noo voo-dree-ohN (zhuh voo-dreh) vwahr
the aquarium.	*l'aquarium.* lah-kwah-ryuhm
the business district.	*le quartier d'affaires.* luh kahr-tyay dah-fehr
the castle.	*le château.* luh shah-to
the cathedral.	*la cathédrale.* lah kah-tay-drahl
the church.	*l'église.* lay-gleez
the downtown.	*le centre-ville.* luh sahNtr-veel
the fountain.	*la fontaine.* lah fohN-tehn
the main square.	*la place principale.* lah plahs praN-see-pahl
the market.	*le marché.* luh mahr-shay
the museum.	*le musée.* luh mew-zay
the old city.	*la vieille ville.* lah vyay veel
the opera.	*l'opéra.* loh-pay-rah
the palace.	*le palais.* luh pah-leh
the park.	*le parc.* luh park
the ruins.	*les ruines.* lay rween
the zoo.	*le zoo.* luh zo
Is there a guided tour?	*Il y a une visite guidée?* eel yah ewn vee-zeet gee-day

continues

At what time?	*À quelle heure?* ah kehl uhr
Where does it leave from?	*D'où part-elle?* doo pahr-tehl
How long does it last?	*Elle dure combien de temps?* ehl dewr kohN-byaN duh tahN
At what time does it return?	*À quelle heure revient la visite?* ah kehl uhr ruh-vyaN lah vee-zeet

General Tourist Admission Information

Is there wheelchair access?	*Il y a un accès pour les chaises roulantes?* eel yah uhN nahks-eh poor lay shez roo-lahNt
Where can I get tickets?	*Où puis-je obtenir des billets?* oo pweezh ohp-tuh-neer day bee-yeh
What days is it open (closed)?	*Quels jours est-il (est-elle) ouvert(e) (fermé[e])?* kehl zhoor eh-teel (eh-tehl) oo-vehr(t) (fehr-may)
At what time does it open (close)?	*À quelle heure ouvre-t-il (-elle)?* ah kehl uhr oo-vruh-teel (-tehl)
What's the admission price?	*Quel est le prix d'entrée?* kehl eh luh pree dahN-tray
Can children enter for free?	*Les enfants peuvent-ils entrer gratuitement?* lay zahN-fahN puhv-teel ahN-tray grah-tweet-mahN
Until what age?	*Jusqu'à quel âge?* zhews-kah kehl ahzh
How much for a child's ticket?	*Quel est le tarif billet enfant?* kehl eh luh tah-reef bee-yeh ahN-fahN

Is there discount for students (seniors)?	*Il y a une réduction de prix pour les étudiants (les seniors)?* eel yah ewn ray-dewks-yohN duh pree poor lay zay-tewd-yahN (lay say-nyohr)
What's the age for seniors?	*À quel âge est-on considéré senior?* ah kehl ahzh eh-tohN kohn-see-day-ray say-nyohr
Is it all right to take pictures (with a flash)?	*Est-il permis de prendre des photos (avec flash)?* eh-teel pehr-mee duh prahNdr day foh-to (ah-vehk flahsh)
Is there a dress code?	*Il y a un code vestimentaire?* eel yah uhN kohd vehs-tee-mahN-tehr
Are there services for people who are disabled (blind) (deaf)?	*Il y a des services pour les personnes handicapées (aveugles) (sourdes)?* eel yah day sehr-vees poor lay pehr-sohn ahN-dee-kah-pay (ah-vuh-gluh) (soord)

Entertainment

Where can I buy ... ?	*Où puis-je acheter ... ?* oo pweezh ahsh-tay
an entertainment guide	*un programme des spectacles* uhN proh-grahm day spehk-tahkl
tickets	*des billets* day bee-yeh
Is it necessary to buy tickets in advance?	*Doit-on acheter les billets à l'avance?* dwah-tohN ahsh-tay lay bee-yeh ah lah-vahNs
Can I buy tickets online?	*Puis-je acheter des billets en ligne?* pweezh ahsh-tay day bee-yeh ahN lee-nyuh

continues

What website gives information?	*Quel site web donne les informations?* kehl seet wehb dohn lay zaN-fohr-mah-syohN
We'd like (I'd like) to go …	*Nous voudrions (Je voudrais) aller …* noo voo-dree-yohN (zhuh voo-dreh) ah-lay
to the amusement park.	*au parc d'attractions.* o pahrk dah-trahk-syohN
to the ballet.	*au ballet.* o bah-leh
to the carnival.	*au carnaval.* o kahr-nah-vahl
to a casino.	*au casino.* o kah-zee-no
to the circus.	*au cirque.* o seerk
to a (rock) (classical music) concert.	*au (de musique rock) (de musique classique) concert.* o (duh mew-seek rohk) (duh mew-seek klah-seek) kohN-sehr
to the fair.	*à la fête foraine.* ah lah feht foh-rehn
to the movies.	*au cinéma.* o see-nay-mah
to the opera.	*à l'opéra.* ah loh-pay-rah
to the theater.	*au théâtre.* o tay-ahtr
Is it far (near)?	*C'est loin (à proximité)?* seh lwaN (ah prohks-ee-mee-tay)
How do I get there?	*Comment puis-je y aller?* koh-mahN pweezh ee ah-lay
What kind of film (play) are they showing?	*Quel genre de film (pièce) jouent-ils?* kehl zhahN-ruh duh feelm (pyehs) zhoo-teel

What's on television?	*Qu'est-ce qu'il y a à la télé?* kehs-keel yah ah lah tay-lay
Is the program in English or in French?	*L'émission, est-elle en anglais ou en français?* lay-mee-syohN eh-tehl ahN nahN-gleh oo ahN frahN-seh
Is it dubbed (in English)?	*Est-il doublé (en anglais)?* eh-teel doo-blay (ahN nahN-gleh)
Are there English subtitles?	*Il y a des sous-titres en anglais?* eel yah des soo-teetr ahN nahN-gleh
What programs are streaming now?	*Quelles émissions sont en streaming maintenant?* kehl zay-mee-syohN sohN tahN stree-meeng maNt-nahN
I'd like to see …	*Je voudrais voir …* zhuh voo-dreh vwahr
an adventure film.	*un film d'aventure.* uhN feelm dah-vahN-tewr
cartoons.	*des dessins animés.* day day-saN ah-nee-may
a comedy.	*une comédie.* ewn koh-may-dee
a documentary.	*un documentaire.* uhN doh-kew-mahN-tehr
a drama.	*un drame.* uhN drahm
a game show.	*un jeu télévisé.* uhN zhuh tay-lay-vee-zay
a horror film.	*un film d'horreur.* uhN feelm doh-ruhr
a love story.	*une histoire d'amour.* ewn ees-twahr dah-moor
a musical.	*une comédie musicale.* ewn koh-may-dee mew-zee-kahl
a mystery.	*un mystère.* uhN mees-tehr

continues

the news.	*les informations.* lay zaN-fohr-mah-syohN
a police story.	*une histoire policière.* ewn ees-twahr poh-lee-syehr
a reality show.	*une émission de téléréalité.* ewn ay-mee-syohN duh tay-lay-ray-ah-lee-tay
a science fiction film.	*un film de science fiction.* uhN feelm duh see-yahNs feek-syohN
a soap opera.	*un feuilleton* *mélodramatique.* uhN fuh-y-tohN may-loh-drah-mah-teek
a spy film.	*un film d'espionnage.* uhN feelm dehs-pyoh-nahzh
a talk show.	*un talk-show.* uhN tohk-sho
the weather.	*la météo.* lah may-tay-o
a Western.	*un western.* uhN wehs-tehrn

Refer to the following explanations when you choose a movie or theater.

INT 18 ans: Interdit aux moins de 18 ans	Forbidden for those under 18 unless accompanied by an adult
V.O.: Version originale	Original version subtitled
V.F.: Version française	Dubbed in French
T.R.: Tarif réduit	Reduced rate

Tickets

Where's the box office (ticket window)?	*Où est le guichet?* oo eh luh gee-sheh
I'd like to pick up my tickets.	*Je voudrais récuperer mes billets.* zhuh voo-dreh ray-koo-pay-ray may bee-yeh
I'd like to purchase tickets for …	*Je voudrais acheter des billets pour …* zhuh voo-dreh ahsh-tay day bee-yeh poor
today.	*aujourd-hui.* o-zhoord-wee
this afternoon (this evening).	*cet après-midi (ce soir).* seh tah-preh-mee-dee (suh swahr)
tomorrow afternoon (tomorrow evening).	*demain après-midi (demain soir).* duh-maN ah-preh-mee-dee (duh-maN swahr)
Are there seats … ?	*Il y a des places … ?* eel yah day plahs
in the orchestra	*à l'orchestre* ah l'ohr-kehstr
in the mezzanine	*au parterre* o pahr-tehr
in the balcony	*au balcon* o bahl-kohN
How much is the ticket?	*C'est combien un billet?* seh kohN-byaN uhN bee-yeh
Are we all sitting together?	*Sommes-nous assis(es) ensemble?* sohm-noo zah-see(z) ahN-sahNbl
Where can I buy a program?	*Où puis-je acheter un programme?* oo pweezh ahsh-tay uhN proh-grahm

Opinions

It was ...	*C'était ...* say-teh
Positive	
awesome.	*génial.* zhay-nyahl
excellent.	*excellent.* ehks-eh-lahN
extraordinary.	*extraordinaire.* ehks-trah-ohr-dee-nehr
fabulous.	*fabuleux.* fah-bew-luh
fun.	*amusant.* ah-mew-zahN
incredible.	*incroyable.* aN-krwah-yahbl
magnificent.	*magnifique.* mah-nyee-feek
marvelous.	*merveilleux.* mehr-veh-yuh
sensational.	*sensationnel.* sahN-sah-syoh-nehl
Negative	
boring.	*ennuyeux.* ahN-nwee-yuh
horrible.	*horrible.* oh-reebl
ridiculous.	*ridicule.* ree-dee-kewl
silly.	*bête.* beht

Active Sports

I like ...	*J'aime bien ...* zhehm byaN
to fish.	*pêcher.* pay-shay
to go hiking.	*faire de la randonnée.* fehr duh lah rahN-doh-nay
to horseback ride.	*monter à cheval.* mohN-tay ah shuh-vahl
to parasail.	*faire du parachute ascensionnel.* fehr dew pah-rah-shoot ah-sahN-syoh-nehl
to play golf.	*jouer au golf.* zoo-ay o gohlf
to play soccer.	*jouer au football.* zhoo-ay o foot-bol
to play tennis.	*jouer au tennis.* zhoo-ay o tay-nees
to play volleyball.	*jouer au volley.* zhoo-ay o voh-leh
to ride a bicycle.	*faire du vélo.* fehr dew vay-lo
to go sailing.	*faire de la voile.* fehr duh lah vwahl
to scuba dive.	*faire de la plongée.* fehr duh lah plohN-zhay
to skate.	*patiner.* pah-tee-nay
to ski.	*faire du ski.* fehr dew skee
to surf.	*faire du surf.* fehr dew soorf
to swim.	*nager.* nah-zhay
to water-ski.	*faire du ski nautique.* fehr dew skee no-teek

continues

| to windsurf. | *faire de la planche à voile.*
fehr duh lah plahNsh ah vwahl |
| to work out. | *faire de l'exercice.*
fehr duh lehks-ehr-sees |

Venues

Where's … ?	*Où est … ?* oo eh
the beach	*la plage* lah plahzh
the field	*le terrain* luh teh-raN
the golf course	*le terrain de golf* luh teh-raN duh gohlf
the gymnasium	*le gymnase* luh zheem-nahz
the mountain	*la montagne* lah mohN-tah-nyuh
the ocean	*l'océan* loh-say-ahN
the park	*le parc* luh pahrk
the pool	*la piscine* lah pee-seen
the rink	*la patinoire* lah pah-tee-nwahr
the sea	*la mer* lah mehr
the slope (ski)	*la piste* lah peest
the tennis court	*le court de tennis* luh koor duh tay-nees
the track	*la piste* lah peest

Equipment

We (I) need … .	*Nous avons (J'ai) besoin de (d') … .* noo zah-vohN (zhay) buh-zwaN duh (d)
Can I borrow … ?	*Puis-je emprunter … ?* pweezh ahN-pruhN-tay
(Where) can I rent … ?	*(Où) Puis-je louer … ?* (oo) pweezh loo-ay
(Where) can I buy … ?	*(Où) Puis-je acheter … ?* oo pweezh ahsh-tay
an air mattress	*un matelas pneumatique* uhN maht-lah pnuh-mah-teek
a ball	*un ballon* uhN bah-lohN
a basketball	*un ballon de basket* uhN bah-lohN duh bahs-keht
a beach ball	*un ballon de plage* uhN bah-lohN duh plahzh
a beach chair	*une chaise de plage* ewn shehz duh plahzh
a beach towel	*une serviette de plage* ewn sehr-vyeht duh plahzh
a beach umbrella	*un parasol* uhN pah-rah-sohl
a bicycle	*un vélo (une bicyclette)* uhN vay-lo (ewn bee-see-kleht)
a boat	*un bateau* uhN bah-to
a canoe	*un canoë* uhN kah-noh-ay
a cooler	*une glacière* ewn glah-syehr
diving equipment	*de l'équipement de plongée* duh lay-keep-mahN duh plohN-zhay

continues

a fishing rod	*une canne à pêche* ewn kahn ah pehsh
golf clubs	*des clubs de golf* day klewb duh gohlf
a helmet	*un casque* uhN kahsk
a racquet	*une raquette* ewn rah-keht
a soccer ball	*un ballon de foot* uhN bah-lohN duh foot
skates	*des patins* day pah-taN
skis (water)	*des skis (nautiques)* day skee (no-teek)
sunglasses	*des lunettes de soleil* day lew-neht duh soh-lehy
sunscreen	*de la crème solaire* duh lah krehm so-lehr
a surfboard	*une planche de surf* ewn plahNsh duh soorf

Spectator Sports

I'd like to see …	*Je voudrais voir …* zhuh voo-dreh vwahr
horse races.	*les courses de chevaux.* lay koors duh shuh-vo
a soccer match.	*un match de football.* uhN mahtch duh foot-bol
a bicycle race.	*une course cycliste.* ewn koors see-kleest
Where's … ?	*Où est … ?* oo eh
the racetrack	*le circuit* luh seer-kwee
the stadium	*le stade* luh stahd

Nightclubs

What's the cover charge?	*C'est combien le couvert?* seh kohN-byaN luh koo-vehr
Is there a minimum?	*Il y a un minimum?* eel yah uhN mee-nee-muhm
Is there dancing?	*On peut danser?* ohN puh dahN-say
At what time does the show start (end)?	*À quelle heure commence (finit) le spectacle?* ah kehl uhr koh-mahNs (fee-nee) luh spehk-tahkl
Do I need to show my ID?	*Dois-je montrer ma carte d'identité?* dwahzh mohN-tray mah kahrt dee-dahN-tee-tay
Is a reservation necessary?	*Faut-il réserver?* fo-teel ray-zehr-vay
We'd like a table near the dance floor.	*Nous voudrions une table près de la piste de danse.* noo voo-dree-yohN ewn tahbl preh duh lah peest duh dahNs

Chapter 12

Medical Care

Falling ill when you're away from home is difficult. The situation becomes even tougher if you can't communicate what's wrong. This chapter provides the phrases you need to explain your ailments and get the help you need.

Medical Services

I don't feel well.	*Je ne me sens pas bien.* zhuh nuh muh sahN pah byaN
I've had an accident.	*J'ai eu un accident.* zhay ew uhN nahks-ee-dahN
Can you recommend a doctor (a specialist) who speaks English?	*Pouvez-vous me recommander un(e) médecin (un[e] spécialiste) qui parle anglais?* poo-vay-voo muh ruh-koh-mahN-day uhN (ewn) mayd-saN (uhN [ewn] spay-syah-leest) kee pahrl ahN-gleh
Where's their office?	*Où est son cabinet?* oo eh sohN kah-bee-neh
Where's the nearest hospital?	*Où est l'hôpital le plus proche?* oo eh lo-pee-tahl luh plew prohsh
How do I get there?	*Comment puis-je y arriver?* kohN-mahN pweezh ee ah-ree-vay
Can someone take me there?	*Quelqu'un peut m'y emmener?* kehl-kuhN puh mee ahNm-nay
Please call for an ambulance.	*Appelez une ambulance s'il vous plaît.* ah-play ewn ahN-bew-lahNs seel voo pleh

Symptoms

My ... hurts.	*... me fait (font) mal.* ... muh feh (fohN) mal
ankle	*Ma cheville ...* mah shuh-vee-y
arm (right) (left)	*Mon bras (droit) (gauche) ...* mohN brah drwah (gosh)

back	*Mon dos ...* mohN do
body	*Mon corps ...* mohN kohr
chest	*Ma poitrine ...* mah pwah-treen
chin	*Mon menton ...* mohN mahN-tohN
ear(s)	*Mon oreille* *(Mes oreilles) ...* mohN noh-reh-y (may zoh-reh-y)
elbow	*Ma coude ...* mah kood
eye(s)	*Mon œil (Mes yeux) ...* mohN nuh-y (may zyuh)
face	*Ma figure ...* mah fee-gewr
finger	*Mon doigt ...* mohN dwah
foot	*Mon pied ...* mohN pyay
forehead	*Mon front ...* mohN frohN
hand	*Ma main ...* mah maN
head	*Ma tête ...* mah teht
hip	*Ma hanche ...* mah ahNsh
knee	*Mon genou ...* mohN zhuh-noo
leg	*Ma jambe ...* mah zhahNb
lips	*Mes lèvres ...* may lehvr
mouth	*Ma bouche ...* mah boosh
neck	*Mon cou ...* mohN koo

continues

nose	*Mon nez ...* mohN nay
shoulder	*Mon épaule ...* mohN nay-pol
stomach	*Mon estomac* *(Mon ventre) ...* mohN nehs-toh-mah (mohN vahNtr)
throat	*Ma gorge ...* mah gohrzh
toe	*Mon doigt de pied ...* mohN dwah duh pyay
tooth	*Ma dent ...* mah dahN
wrist	*Mon poignet ...* mohN pwah-neh
I have ...	*J'ai ...* zhay
a backache.	*mal au dos.* mahl o do
a blister.	*une ampoule.* ewn ahN-pool
a bruise (a hematoma).	*un bleu (une hématome).* uhN bluh (ewn ay-mah-tohm)
a burn.	*une brûlure.* ewn brew-lewr
chills.	*des frissons.* (m.) day free-sohN
a cold.	*un rhume.* uhN rewm
a cough.	*une toux.* ewn too
cramps.	*des crampes.* (f.) day krahNp
a cut.	*une coupure.* ewn koo-pewr
diarrhea.	*la diarrhée.* lah dyah-ray
an earache.	*mal aux oreilles.* mahl o zoh-reh-y

a fever.	*une fièvre.* ewn fyehvr
indigestion.	*une indigestion.* ewn aN-dee-zhehs-tyohN
a lump.	*une grosseur.* ewn gro-suhr
a migraine.	*une migraine.* ewn mee-grehn
a rash.	*des rougeurs.* (f.) day roo-zhuhr
a sore throat.	*mal à la gorge.* mahl ah lah gohrzh
a stomachache.	*mal à l'estomac* *(au ventre).* mahl ah lehs-toh-mah (o vahNtr)
swelling.	*une enflure.* ewn ahN-flewr
a wound.	*une blessure.* ewn bleh-sewr
I've lost my sense of taste (smell).	*J'ai perdu le goût (l'odorat).* zhay pehr-dew luh goo (loh-doh-rah)
I have a pain in my foot.	*J'ai mal au pied.* zhay mahl o pyay
I feel a (sharp) pain here.	*J'ai une douleur (vive) ici.* zhay ewn doo-luhr veev ee-see
Do I have … ?	*Est-ce que j'ai … ?* ehs-kuh zhay
a broken bone	*un os cassé* uhN nohs kah-say
a fracture	*une fracture* ewn frahk-tewr
a sprain	*une entorse* ewn ahN-tohrs
I'm bleeding.	*Je saigne.* zhuh seh-nyuh
I'm constipated.	*Je suis constipé(e).* zhuh swee kohN-stee-pay
I'm coughing.	*Je tousse.* zhuh toos

continues

I'm dizzy.	*J'ai le vertige.* zhay luh vehr-teezh
I'm exhausted.	*Je suis épuisé(e).* zhuh swee zay-pwee-zay
I'm nauseous.	*J'ai mal au cœur.* zhay mahl o kuhr
I'm sneezing.	*J'éternue.* zhay-tehr-new
I vomited.	*J'ai vomi.* zhay voh-mee
I can't sleep.	*Je ne peux pas dormir.* zhuh nuh puh pah dohr-meer
I can't breathe.	*Je ne peux pas respirer.* zhuh nuh puh pah rehs-pee-ray
I hurt everywhere.	*J'ai mal partout.* zhay mahl pahr-too
I feel weak.	*Je me sens faible.* zhuh muh sahN fehbl
Do I have COVID symptoms?	*Est-ce que j'ai des symptômes de COVID?* ehs-kuh zhay day saNp-tom duh koh-veed
I've felt this way since …	*Je me sens ainsi depuis …* zhuh muh sahN zaN-see duh-pwee
last week.	*la semaine dernière.* lah suh-mehn dehr-nyehr
the day before yesterday.	*avant-hier.* ah-vahN-yehr
yesterday.	*hier.* yehr
last night.	*hier soir.* yehr swahr
this morning.	*ce matin.* suh mah-taN
this afternoon.	*cet après-midi.* seh tah-preh-mee-dee

I fell.	*Je suis tombé(e).* zhuh swee tohN-bay
I fainted.	*Je me suis évanoui(e).* zhuh muh swee zay-vahn-wee
I cut myself.	*Je me suis coupé(e).* zhuh muh swee koo-pay
I burned myself.	*Je me suis brûlé(e).* zhuh muh swee brew-lay
An insect bit me.	*Un insecte m'a piqué(e).* uhN naN-sehk mah pee-kay
A dog bit me.	*Un chien m'a mordu(e).* uhN shyaN mah mohr-dew
I'm (not) allergic …	*Je (ne) suis (pas)* *allergique …* zhuh (nuh) swee (pahz) ah-lehr-zheek
to antibiotics.	*aux antibiotiques.* o zahN-tee-byoh-teek
to anti-inflammatories.	*aux anti-inflammatoires.* o zahN-tee-aN-flah-mah-twahr
to bee stings.	*aux piqûres d'abeille.* o pee-kewr dah-beh-y
to latex.	*au latex.* o lah-tehks
to peanuts.	*aux cacahuètes.* o kah-kah-weht
to penicillin.	*à la pénicilline.* ah lah pay-nee-see-leen
to pollen.	*au pollen.* o poh-lehn
to shellfish.	*aux crustacés.* o krew-stah-say
I have an adverse reaction to painkillers.	*J'ai une réaction défavorable* *aux analgésiques.* zhay ewn ray-ahks-yohN day-fah-foh-rahbl o zah-nahl-zhay-zeek

Medical History

I had ...	*J'ai eu ...* zhay ew
back surgery ...	*une opération du dos ...* ewn oh-pay-rah-syohN dew do
(triple) (quadruple) bypass surgery ...	*un pontage (triple) (quadruple) ...* uhN pohN-ahzh (treepl) kwah-droopl)
cancer ...	*le cancer ...* luh kahN-sehr
chemotherapy ...	*la chimiothérapie ...* lah shee-myoh-tay-rah-pee
a heart attack ...	*une crise cardiaque ...* ewn kreez kahr-dyahk
a heart transplant ...	*une greffe du cœur ...* ewn grehf dew kuhr
a (right) (left) kidney transplant ...	*une greffe de rein (droit) (gauche) ...* ewn grehf duh raN (drwah) (gosh)
a liver transplant ...	*une greffe de foie ...* ewn grehf duh fwah
radiation ...	*la radiothérapie ...* lah rah-dyoh-tay-rah-pee
a stroke ...	*un accident vasculaire cérébral ...* uhN nahks-ee-dahN vah-skew-lehr say-ray-brahl
... years ago.	*il y a ... ans.* eel yah ... ahN
I have ...	*J'ai ...* zhay
AIDS.	*le SIDA.* luh see-dah
cancer.	*le cancer.* luh kahN-sehr
Crohn's.	*la maladie de Crohn.* lah mah-lah-dee de krohn

diabetes.	*le diabète.* luh dyah-beht
hay fever.	*le rhume des foins.* luh rewm day fwaN
high blood pressure.	*l'hypertension.* (f.) lee-pehr-tahN-syohN
high cholesterol.	*un taux de cholestérol élevé.* uhN to duh koh-lehs-tay-rohl ay-lvay
multiple sclerosis.	*la sclérose en plaques.* lah sklay-roz ahN plahk
Parkinson's disease.	*la maladie de Parkinson.* lah mah-lah-dee duh Parkinson
I take these medications: …	*Je prends ces médicaments: …* zhuh prahN say may-dee-kah-mahN
I'm pregnant.	*Je suis enceinte(e).* zhuh swee zahN-saNt
I smoke. (I don't smoke.)	*Je fume. (Je ne fume pas.)* zhuh fewm (zhuh fewm nuh pah)
I take drugs. (I don't take drugs.)	*Je prends de la drogue.* *(Je ne prends pas de drogue.)* zhuh prahN duh lah drohg (zhuh nuh prahN pah duh drohg)
I drink alcohol. (I don't drink alcohol.)	*Je bois de l'alcool.* *(Je ne bois pas d'alcool.)* zhuh bwah duh lahl-kohl (zhuh nuh bwah pah dahl-kohl)
I had … removed.	*J'ai eu … retiré(e).* zhay ew … ruh-tee-ray
my appendix	*mon appendice* mohN nah-pahN-dees
my gall bladder	*ma vésicule biliaire* mah vay-see-kewl bee-lyehr
my (right) (left) kidney	*mon rein (droit) (gauche)* mohN raN (drwah) (gosh)
my (right) (left) lung	*mon poumon (droit) (gauche)* mohN poo-mohN (drwah) (gosh)

continues

my spleen	*ma rate* mah raht
my thyroid	*ma thyroïde* mah tee-roh-eed
I've had a hysterectomy.	*J'ai eu une hystérectomie.* zhay ew ewn ees-tay-rehk-toh-mee
I've had the ... vaccine (recently).	*J'ai eu le vaccin contre ...* *(récemment).* zhay ew luh vahk-saN kohNtr ... ray-seh-mahN
COVID	*la COVID* lah koh-veed
diphtheria	*la diphtérie* lah deef-tay-ree
flu	*la grippe* lah greep
hepatitis	*l'hépatite* (f.) lay-pah-teet
measles	*la rougeole* lah roo-zhohl
MMR	*le ROR* luh ehr-o-ehr
polio	*la polio* lah poh-lyo
pneumonia	*la pneumonie* lah pnuh-moh-nee
rabies	*la rage* lah rahzh
rubella	*la rubéole* lah roo-bay-ohl
shingles	*le zona* luh zo-nah
tetanus	*le tétanos* luh tay-tah-nos
typhoid	*la typhoïde* lah tee-foh-eed
There's a (There's no) ... in my family.	*Il y a (Il n'y a pas de) ...* *dans ma famille.* eel yah (eel nyah pah duh) ... dahN mah fah-mee-y

Diagnosis

What's wrong?	*Qu'est-ce qui ne va pas?* kehs-kee nuh vah pah
Is it serious (contagious)?	*Est-ce grave (contagieux)?* ehs grahv (kohN-tah-zhyuh)
Are you going to give me a prescription?	*Allez-vous me donner une ordonnance?* ah-lay-voo muh doh-nay ewn ohr-doh-nahNs
How many times per day must I take this medicine?	*Je dois prendre ce médicament combien de fois par jour?* zhuh dwah prahNdr suh may-dee-kah-mahN kohN-byaN duh fwah pahr zhoor
(How long) Do I have to stay in bed?	*(Pendant combien de temps) Dois-je rester au lit?* (pahN-dahN kohN-byaN duh tahN) dwahzh rehs-tay o lee
When can I continue to travel?	*Quand puis-je continuer à voyager?* kahN pweezh kohN-tee-new-ay ah vwah-yah-zhay
How much do I owe you?	*Je vous dois combien?* zhuh voo dwah kohN-byan
May I please have a receipt for my medical insurance?	*Puis-je avoir un reçu pour mon assurance médicale s'il vous plaît?* pweezh ah-vwahr uhN ruh-sew poor mohN nah-sew-rahNs may-dee-kahl seel voo pleh

At the Pharmacy

A green cross indicates a pharmacy (*une pharmacie* [ewn fahr-mah-see]), which sells over-the-counter and prescription medication, personal hygiene items, and some cosmetics.

Une droguerie (ewn drohg-ree) sells paints, chemical products, household cleansers and accessories (such as mops, brooms, buckets), and some hygiene and beauty products. It doesn't dispense prescriptions.

Un drugstore (uhN druhg-stohr) resembles a small department store that offers personal hygiene items, books, magazines, newspapers, guides, maps, gifts, and souvenirs—but not prescription medicine. (In Canada, a "drugstore" more resembles the kind you'd see in the United States.)

Where's the nearest (all-night) pharmacy?	*Où se trouve la pharmacie (de garde) (de nuit) la plus proche?* oo suh troov lah fahr-mah-see (duh gahrd) (duh nwee) lah plew prohsh
Where's a compound pharmacy located?	*Où se trouve une pharmacie réalisant des préparations magistrales?* oo suh troov ewn fahr-mah-see ray-ah-lee-zahN day pray-pah-rah-syohN mah-zhees-trahl
At what time does it open (close)?	*À quelle heure ouvre-(ferme-)t-elle?* ah kehl uhr oovr- (fehrm-)tehl
Is a prescription needed?	*Faut-il avoir une ordonnance?* fo-teel ah-vwahr ewn ohr-doh-nahNs
Here it is.	*La voilà.* lah vwah-lah

Could you fill this prescription (immediately)?	*Pourriez-vous préparer cette ordonnance (immédiatement)?* poo-ryay-voo pray-pah-ray seht ohr-doh-nahNs (ee-may-dyaht-mahN)
How long will it take?	*Ça va prendre combien de temps?* sah vah prahNdr kohN-byaN duh tahN
Can I wait here?	*Puis-je attendre ici?* pweezh ah-tahNdr ee-see
How many pills do I take per day?	*Combien de pilules dois-je prendre par jour?* kohN-byaN duh pee-lewl dwahzh prahNdr pahr zhoor
For how many days?	*Pour combien de jours?* poor kohN-byaN duh zhoor
How does one take this medicine?	*Comment prend-on ce médicament?* koh-mahN prahN-tohN suh may-dee-kah-mahN
With or without food?	*Avec ou sans nourriture?* ah-vehk oo sahN noo-ree-tewr
Will these pills make me drowsy?	*Est-ce que ces pilules me rendront somnolent(e)?* ehs-kuh say pee-lewl muh rahN-drohN sohm-noh-lahN(t)
Will they keep me awake?	*Est-ce qu'elles m'empêcheront de dormir?* ehs-kehl mahN-pehsh-rohN duh dohr-meer
What are the side effects?	*Quels sont les effets secondaires?* kehl sohN lay zay-feh suh-gohN-dehr
Are there any contraindications?	*Il y a des contre-indications?* eel yah day kohNtr-aN-dee-kah-syohN
Do you sell the morning-after pill?	*Vendez-vous la pilule du lendemain?* vahN-day-voo lah pee-lewl dew lahNd-maN

continues

I'm looking for …	*Je cherche …* zhuh shehrsh
after-shave lotion.	*de la lotion après-rasage.* duh lah lo-syohN ah-preh-rah-zahzh
alcohol.	*de l'alcool.* (m.) duh lahl-kohl
an antacid.	*un anti-acide.* uhN nahN-tee-ah-seed
an antihistamine.	*un antihistaminique.* uhN nahN-tee-ees-tah- mee-neek
an antiseptic.	*un antiseptique.* uhN nahN-tee-sehp-teek
aspirins.	*des aspirines.* (f.) day zahs-pee-reen
a baby bottle.	*un biberon.* uhN bee-brohN
a bandage.	*un pansement.* uhN pahNs-mahN
Band-Aids.	*des pansements adhésifs.* (m.) day pahNs-mahN ahd-ay-zeef
blush.	*du fard à joues.* dew fahr ah zhoo
bobby pins.	*des pinces* [f.] *à cheveux.* day paNs ah shuh-vuh
a brush.	*une brosse.* ewn brohs
cleansing cream.	*de la crème démaquillante.* duh lah krehm day-mah-kee-yahNt
a comb.	*un peigne.* uhN peh-nyuh
condoms.	*des préservatifs.* (m.) day pray-zehr-vah-teef
cotton.	*du coton.* dew koh-tohN

cough drops.	*des pastilles contre la toux.* (f.) day pahs-tee-y kohNtr lah too
cough syrup.	*du sirop contre la toux.* dew see-ro kohNtr lah too
deodorant.	*du déodorant.* dew day-oh-doh-rahN
(disposable) diapers.	*des couches (jetables).* (f.) day koosh (zhuh-tahbl)
ear drops.	*des gouttes* [f.] *pour les oreilles.* day goot poor lay zoh-reh-y
eye drops.	*des gouttes* [f.] *pour les yeux.* day goot poor lay zyuh
eye shadow.	*du fard à paupières.* dew fahr ah po-pyehr
an eyebrow pencil.	*un crayon à sourcils.* uhN kreh-yohN ah soor-see
an eyeliner.	*un eye-liner.* uhN nahy-lahy-nehr
a first-aid kit.	*une trousse de premiers secours.* ewn troos duh pruh-myay suh-koor
foundation.	*du fond de teint.* dew fohN duh taN
gauze.	*du coton hydrophile.* dew koh-tohN ee-droh-feel
gel.	*du gel.* dew zhehl
hairspray.	*de la laque.* duh lah lahk
hand sanitizer.	*du désinfectant pour les mains.* dew day-zaN-fehk-tahN poor lay maN
hand wipes.	*des lingettes.* (f.) day laN-zheht

continues

a heating pad.	*une compresse chauffante.* ewn kohN-prehs sho-fahNt
an ice pack.	*une poche de glace.* ewn pohsh duh glahs
a laxative.	*un laxatif.* uhN lahks-ah-teef
a lipstick.	*un rouge à lèvres.* uhN roozh ah lehvr
makeup.	*du maquillage.* dew mah-kee-yahzh
mascara.	*du mascara.* dew mahs-kah-rah
milk of magnesia.	*du lait de magnésie.* dew leh duh mah-nyay-zee
a mirror.	*un miroir.* uhN mee-rwahr
moisturizer.	*de la crème hydratante.* duh lah krehm ee-drah-tahNt
mousse.	*de la mousse coiffante.* duh lah moos kwah-fahNt
mouthwash.	*un bain de bouche.* uhN baN duh boosh
nail clippers.	*un coupe-ongles.* uhN koop-ohNgl
a nail file (an emory board).	*des limes* [f.] *à ongles.* day leem ah ohNgl
nail polish.	*du vernis à ongles.* dew vehr-nee ah ohNgl
nail polish remover.	*du dissolvant.* dew dee-sohl-vahN
nose drops.	*des gouttes* [f.] *pour le nez.* day goot poor luh nay
a pacifier.	*une tétine.* ewn tay-teen
a (disposable) razor.	*un rasoir (jetable).* uhN rah-zwahr (zhuh-tahbl)
an (electric) razor.	*un rasoir (électrique).* uhN rah-zwahr ay-lehk-treek

razor blades.	*des lames* [f.] *de rasoir.* day lahm duh rah-zwahr
safety pins.	*des épingles* [f.] *à nourrice.* day zay-paNgl ah noo-rees
(menstrual) pads.	*des serviettes* [f.] *hygiéniques.* day sehr-vyeht ee-zhyay-neek
scissors.	*des ciseaux.* (m.) day see-zo
shampoo (anti-dandruff).	*du shampooing* *(antipelliculaire).* dew shahN-pwaN (ahN-tee-peh-lee-kew-lehr)
shaving cream.	*de la crème à raser.* duh lah krehm ah rah-zay
sleeping pills.	*des somnifères.* (m.) day sohm-nee-fehr
soap (a bar of).	*une savonnette.* ewn sah-voh-neht
sunscreen.	*de la crème solaire.* duh lah krehm so-lehr
syringes.	*des seringues.* (f.) day suh-raNg
tampons.	*des tampons* *(hygiéniques).* (m.) day tahN-pohN (ee-zhyay-neek
a thermometer.	*un thermomètre.* uhN tehr-moh-mehtr
tissues.	*des mouchoirs* [m.] *en papier.* day moo-shwahr ahN pah-pyay
a toothbrush.	*une brosse à dents.* ewn brohs ah dahN
toothpaste.	*du dentifrice.* dew dahN-tee-frees
vitamins.	*des vitamines.* (f.) day vee-tah-meen

continues

At the Dentist

Could you recommend me a good dentist?	*Pourriez-vous me recommander un bon dentiste?* poo-ryay-voo muh ruh-koh-mahN-day uhN bohN dahN-teest
Where's their office?	*Où se trouve son cabinet?* oo suh troov sohN kah-bee-neh
I have a toothache.	*J'ai un mal de dents.* zhay uhN mahl duh dahN
I think I have a cavity.	*Je crois que j'ai une carie.* zhuh krwah kuh zhay uhN kah-ree
I've broken a tooth.	*Ma dent s'est cassée.* mah dahN seh kah-say
My filling fell out.	*J'ai perdu un plombage.* zhay pehr-dew uhN plohN-bahzh
My crown fell off.	*J'ai perdu une couronne.* zhay pehr-dew ewn koo-rohn
Can you fix it temporarily?	*Pouvez-vous le (la) réparer temporairement?* poo-vay-voo luh (lah) ray-pah-ray tahN-poh-rehr-mahN
Can you fix … ?	*Pouvez-vous réparer … ?* poo-vay-voo ray-pah-ray
this bridge	*ce bridge* suh breedzh
this crown	*cette couronne* seht koo-rohn
these dentures	*ce dentier* suh dahN-tyay
this implant	*cet implant* seh taN-plahN
this tooth	*cette dent* seht dahN
Will you have to pull this tooth?	*Faut-il arracher cette dent?* fo-teel ah-rah-shay seht dahN

Do I need a root canal?	*Il me faut un traitement radiculaire?* eel muh fo tuhN treht-mahN rah-dee-kew-lehr
Is there an infection (an abscess)?	*Il y a une infection (un abcès)?* eel yah ewn aN-fehk-syohN (uhN nahb-seh)
My gums hurt.	*Les gencives me font mal.* lay zhahN-seev muh fohN mahl
(When) Do I have to come back?	*(Quand) Dois-je revenir?* (kahN) dwahzh ruh-vuh-neer
How much do I owe you?	*Je vous dois combien?* zhuh voo dwah kohN-byaN

**Chapter
13**

Banking, Business & Technology

Conducting business in a foreign country can be challenging. It's crucial to know how to exchange money, perform certain banking transactions, arrange business meetings, place phone calls, send emails or texts, buy stationery items, and work with ever-changing technologies. This chapter will help you with all these situations and more.

Banking

Major credit and debit cards are accepted in most establishments throughout the French-speaking world. You'll likely need some cash for small expenses. It's therefore a good idea to exchange some money before your arrival despite the fact you won't get the best rate.

You will, though, get the best exchange rate if you wait until you arrive at your destination. Major airports have a currency exchange desk, but you'll probably get a better rate from an ATM affiliated with a major bank.

Un bureau de change (uhN bew-ro duh shahNzh) also exchanges money. Some offer terrific exchange rates, whereas others charge exorbitant commissions. It's always a good idea to investigate a few before making a transaction.

Currency Exchange

Where's the nearest money exchange?	*Où est le bureau de change le plus proche?* oo eh luh bew-ro duh shahNzh luh plew prohsh
When does it open (close)?	*Quand ouvre (ferme)-t-il?* kahNd oovr-teel (fehrm)-teel)
Where's the nearest bank?	*Où est trouve la banque la plus proche?* oo eh troov lah bahNk lah plew prohsh
What are the business hours?	*Quelles sont les heures d'ouverture?* kehl sohN lay zuhr doo-vehr-tewr

What's the current exchange rate?	*Quel est le taux de change actuel?* kehl eh luh to duh shahNzh ahk-twehl
Do you have an ATM?	*Avez-vous un distributeur automatique de billets?* ah-vay voo ewn dees-tree-bew-tuhr o-toh-mah-teek duh bee-yay
Where's it located?	*Où est-il situé?* oo eh-teel see-tew-ay
How does one use it?	*Comment s'en servir?* koh-mahN sahN sehr-veer
Is it available all the time?	*Est-il disponible tout le temps?* eh-teel dees-poh-neebl too luh tahN
Can I take my money out 24 hours a day?	*Puis-je retirer mon argent vingt-quatre heures sur vingt-quatre?* pweezh ruh-tee-ray mohN nahr-zhahN vaN-kahtr uhr sewr vaN-kahtr
Are there transaction fees?	*Y a-t-il des frais d'utilisation?* ee ah-teel day freh dew-tee-lee-zah-syohN
How much is it for each transaction?	*C'est combien pour chaque transaction?* seh kohN-byaN poor shahk trahN-zahks-syohN
The ATM ...	*Le distributeur ...* luh dees-tree-bew-tuhr
didn't give me enough money.	*ne m'a pas donné assez d'argent.* nuh mah pah doh-nay ah-say dahr-zhahN
gave me too much money.	*m'a donné trop d'argent.* mah doh-nay tro dahr-zhahN
swallowed my card.	*a avalé ma carte.* ah ah-vah-lay mah kahrt
Can I cash a personal check?	*Puis-je toucher un chèque personnel?* pweezh too-shay uhN shehk pehr-soh-nehl

continues

I'd like to change some money.	*Je voudrais changer de l'argent.* zhuh voo-dreh shahN-zhay duh lahr-zhahN
I'd like the money in (large) (small) bills.	*Je voudrais l'argent en (grosses) (petites) coupures.* zhuh voo-dreh lahr-zhahN ahN (gros) (puh-teet) koo-pewr
What's the commission rate?	*Quel est le taux de commission?* kehl eh luh to duh koh-mee-syohN
Please give me a receipt.	*Donnez-moi un reçu s'il vous plaît.* doh-nay mwah uhN ruh-sew seel voo pleh
I'd like to take a cash advance on my credit card.	*Je voudrais prendre une avance de fonds de ma carte de crédit.* zhuh voo-dreh prahNdr ewn ah-vahNs duh fohN duh mah kahrt duh kray-dee
I'd like to withdraw money using my debit card.	*Je voudrais retirer de l'argent en employant ma carte de débit.* zhuh voo-dreh ruh-tee-ray duh lahr-zhahN ahN nahN-plwah-yahN mah kahrt duh day-bee

Banking Words & Expressions

bank branch	*l'agence bancaire* (f.) lah-zhahN bahN-kehr
cash	*les espèces* (f.) *(l'argent liquide)* [m.] lay zehs-pehs (lahr-zhahN lee-keed)
to cash	*toucher* too-shay
cashier	*le caissier (la caissière)* luh keh-syay (lah keh-syehr)

change (coins)	*la monnaie* lah moh-neh
to change (transaction)	*échanger* ay-shahN-zhay
check	*le chèque* luh shehk
coin	*la pièce de monnaie* lah pyehs duh moh-neh
currency (foreign)	*les devises* [f.] *(la monnaie)* *(étrangère[s])* lay duh-veez (lah moh-neh) (ay-trahN-zhehr)
employee	*l'employé(e)* lahN-plwah-yay
to endorse	*endosser* ahN-doh-say
exchange rate	*le taux de change* luh to duh shahNzh
to fill out	*remplir* rahN-pleer
PIN	*le code confidentiel* luh kohd kohN-fee-dahN-syehl
receipt	*le reçu* luh ruh-sew
to sign	*signer* see-nyay
signature	*la signature* lah see-nyah-tewr
sum	*la somme* lah sohm
teller	*le guichetier (la guichetière)* luh geesh-tyay (lah geesh-tyehr)
teller window	*le guichet* luh gee-sheh
void	*non valable* nohN vah-lahbl

Conducting Business

I'm here on business.	*Je suis ici en voyage d'affaires.* zhuh swee zee-see ahN vwah-yahzh dah-fehr
Where's the meeting (the conference)?	*Où est la réunion (la conférence)?* oo eh lah ray-ew-nyohN (lah kohN-fay-rahNs)
At what time is the (emergency) meeting?	*À quelle heure est la réunion (d'urgence)?* ah kehl uhr eh lah ray-ew-nyohN (dewr-zhahNs)
The meeting is at 9 a.m. sharp.	*La réunion a lieu à neuf heures précises du matin.* lah ray-ew-nyohN ah lyuh ah nuh vuhr pray-seez dew mah-taN
Do I need a name tag?	*Est-ce que j'ai besoin d'un badge (un insigne d'identification)?* ehs-kuh zhay buh-zwaN duhN bahdzh (uhN naN-see-nyuh dee-dahN-tee-fee-kah-syohN)
Where should I sit?	*Où dois-je m'asseoir?* oo dwahzh mah-swahr
Who's speaking?	*Qui parle?* kee pahrl
What topic are we discussing?	*De quel sujet discutons-nous?* duh kehl sew-zheh dees-kew-tohN-noo
I have a meeting (appointment) with ...	*J'ai un rendez-vous avec ...* zhay uhN rahN-day-voo ah-vehk
the auditor.	*l'auditeur (l'auditrice).* lo-dee-tuhr (lo-dee-trees)
the bookeeper (accountant).	*le (la) comptable.* luh (lah) kohN-tahbl

the CEO.	*le (la) PDG (le président-directeur général [la présidente-directrice générale]).* luh (lah) pay-day-zhay (luh pray-zee-dahN-dee-rehk-tuhr zhay-nay-rahl [lah pray-zee-dahNt-dee-rehk-trees zhay-nay-rahl])
the CFO.	*e (la) DEF (le directeur financier [la directrice financière]).* luh (lah) day-uh-ehf (luh dee-rehk-tuhr fee-nahN-syay [lah dee-rehk-trees fee-nahN-syehr])
the COO.	*le directeur (la directrice) des opérations.* luh dee-rehk-tuhr (lah dee-rehk-trees) day zoh-pay-rah-syohN
the president.	*le (la) président(e).* luh (lah) pray-zee-dahN(t)
the vice president.	*le (la) vice-président(e).* luh (lah) vees-pray-zee-dahN(t)
the head of marketing.	*le directeur (la directrice) de marketing.* luh dee-rehk-tuhr (lah dee-rehk-trees) duh mahr-keh-teeng
the lawyer(s).	*les avocat(e)(s).* lay zah-voh-kah(t)
the owner.	*le (la) propriétaire.* luh (lah) proh-pree-yay-tehr
Where's his/her (their) office?	*Où est son (leur) bureau?* oo eh sohN (luhr) bew-ro
I need (I don't need) an interpreter.	*J'ai besoin (Je n'ai pas besoin) d'un interprète.* zhay buh-zwaN (zhuh nay pah buh-zwaN) duhN naN-tehr-preht

continues

Here's my business card.	*Voici ma carte de visite.* vwah-see mah kahrt duh vee-zeet
Please give me your business card.	*Donnez-moi votre carte* *de visite s'il vous plait.* doh-nay mwah vohtr kahrt duh vee-zeet seel voo pleh
I've prepared a PowerPoint presentation.	*J'ai préparé une présentation* *PowerPoint.* zhay pray-pah-ray ewn pray- zahN-tah-syohN PowerPoint
Please look at the data on this spreadsheet.	*Regardez les données sur cette* *feuille de calcul.* ruh-gahr-day lay doh-nay sewr seht fuh-y duh kahl-kewl
Do you have any questions?	*Avez-vous des questions?* ah-vay voo day kehs-tyohN
Here's a catalog (the price list) of our products	*Voici une catalogue (le tarif)* *de nos produits.* vwah-see ewn kah-tah-lohg (luh tah-reef) duh no proh-dwee
Do you have a catalog of your products?	*Avez-vous une catalogue* *de vos produits?* ah-vay-voo ewn kah-tah-lohg duh vo proh-dwee
Do you have a price list for your products?	*Avez-vous le tarif de vos* *produits?* ah-vay-voo luh tah-reef duh vo proh-dwee
Can you demonstrate how this product works?	*Pouvez-vous démontrer* *comment ce produit* *fonctionne?* poo-vay-voo day-mohN-tray koh-mahN suh proh-dwee fohNk-syohn
Marketing strategy is a top priority.	*La stratégie marketing* *est une priorité absolue.* lah strah-tay-zhee mahr-keh- teeng eh tewn pree-oh-ree-tay ahp-soh-lew

Do you have any (free) marketing materials (free samples)?	*Avez-vous des brochures commerciales (gratuites) (échantillons gratuits)?* ah-vay-voo day broh-shewr koh-mehr-syahl (grah-tweet) (ay-shahN-tee-yohN grah-twee)
Could you give me any (free) samples?	*Pourriez-vous me donner des échantillons (gratuits)?* poor-yay voo muh doh-nay day zay-shahN-tee-yohN (grah-twee)
Please send me an invoice.	*Envoyez-moi une facture s'il vous plaît.* ahN-vwah-yay mwah ewn fahk-tewr seel voo pleh
Are the contracts ready?	*Les contrats sont prêts?* lay kohN-trah sohN preh
I need … my boss.	*Je dois … à mon patron (ma patronne).* zhuh dwah … ah mohN pah-trohN (mah pah-trohn)
to call	*téléphoner* tay-lay-foh-nay
to email	*envoyer un email* ahN-vwah-yay uhN ee-mehl
to text	*envoyer un texto* ahN-vwah-yay uhN tehks-to
We have a permanent (temporary) contract.	*Nous avons un contrat permanent (temporaire).* noo zah-vohN zuhN kohN-trah pehr-mah-nahN (tahN-poh-rehr)
Where do I sign?	*Où dois-je signer?* oo dwahzh see-nyay
We need more time.	*Il nous faut plus de temps.* eel noo fo plew duh tahN

Making a Phone Call

I'll call you soon.	*Je vous téléphonerai bientôt.* zhuh voo tay-lay-fohn-ray byaN-to
I'll get back to you.	*Je vous rappellerai.* zhuh voo rah-pehl-ray

continues

What's your (cell) phone number?	*Quel est votre numéro de téléphone (portable) (mobile) (cellulaire)?* kehl eh vohtr new-may-ro duh tay-lay-fohn (pohr-tahbl) (moh-beel) (seh-lew-lehr)
I'll text you.	*Je vous enverrai un texto.* zhuh voo zahN-vay-ray uhN tehks-to
My number is … .	*Mon numéro est … .* mohN new-may-ro eh
Do you have an answering machine?	*Avez-vous un répondeur?* ah-vay-voo uhN ray-pohN-duhr
May I leave a message?	*Puis-je laisser un message?* pweezh lay-say uhN meh-sahzh
Where's … ?	*Où se trouve … ?* oo suh troov
a public phone	*un téléphone public* uhN tay-lay-fohn pew-bleek
a phone book	*un téléphonique annuaire* uhN tay-lay-fohn nahN-wehr
May I use your phone (cell phone)?	*Puis-je utiliser votre téléphone (portable)?* pweezh ew-tee-lee-zay vohtr tay-lay-fohn (pohr-tahbl)
Where can I buy … ?	*Où puis-je acheter … ?* oo pweezh ahsh-tay
a prepaid phone card	*une carte téléphonique prépayée?* ewn kahrt tay-lay-foh-neek pray-pay-ay
a prepaid cell phone	*un portable prépayé?* uhN pohr-tahbl pray-pay-ay
Do you have a cell phone charger?	*Avez-vous un chargeur de téléphone portable?* ah-vay-voo uhN shahr-zhuhr duh tay-lay-fohn pohr-tahbl
May I borrow it?	*Puis-je l'emprunter?* pweezh lahN-pruhN-tay
May I use it?	*Puis-je l'utiliser?* pweezh lew-tee-lee-zay

Hello. This is … .	*Allô. Ici … .* ah-lo ee-see
May I speak to … ?	*Puis-je parler à … ?* pweezh pahr-lay ah
Please speak louder (slower).	*Parlez plus fort (lentement) s'il vous plaît.* pahr-lay plew fohr (lahNt-mahN) seel voo pleh
Don't hang up.	*Ne quittez pas.* nuh kee-tay pah
Sorry, I have the wrong number.	*Pardon, j'ai le mauvais numéro.* pahr-dohN zhay luh mo-veh new-may-ro
We got cut off (disconnected).	*On nous a coupé(e)s.* ohN noo zah koo-pay
There's a lot of static.	*Il y a beaucoup de parasites.* eel yah bo-koo duh pah-rah-seet
I can't hear you.	*Je ne peux pas vous entendre.* zhuh nuh puh pah voo zahN-tahNdr
I have to charge my phone.	*Je dois recharger mon portable.* zhuh dwah ruh-shahr-zhay mohN pohr-tahbl
Where can I do it?	*Où puis-je le faire?* oo pweezh luh fehr
I'll call you back.	*Je vous rappellerai.* zhuh voo rah-pehl-ray

Business Words & Expressions

accountant	*le (la) comptable* luh (lah) kohN-tahbl
assets	*les actifs* (m.) *(le capital)* lay zahk-teef (luh kah-pee-tahl)
to authorize	*autoriser* o-toh-ree-zay
a bargain	*une bonne affaire* ewn bohn ah-fehr

continues

bill	*la facture* lah fahk-tewr
bill of sale	*l'acte de vente* (m.) lahkt duh vahNt
bookkeeping	*la comptabilité* lah kohN-tah-bee-lee-tay
business	*les affaires* (f.) lay zah-fehr
to buy	*acheter* ahsh-tay
to buy at auction	*acheter aux enchères* ahsh-tay o zahN-shehr
to buy for cash	*payer en argent comptant* pay-yay ahN nahr-zhahN kohN-tahN
to buy on credit	*acheter à crédit* ahsh-tay ah kray-dee
a buyout	*un rachat* uhN rah-shah
to buy out (take over ownership)	*racheter* rahsh-tay
to cash a check	*toucher un chèque* too-shay uhN shehk
competitive price	*le prix compétitif* luh pree kohN-pay-tee-teef
consumer	*le consommateur* *(la consommatrice)* luh kohN-soh-mah-tuhr (lah kohN-soh-mah-trees)
contract	*le contrat* luh kohN-trah
credit	*le crédit* luh kray-dee
debit	*le débit* luh day-bee
to deliver	*livrer* lee-vray
discount	*la remise (la réduction)* lah ruh-meez (lah ray-dewk-syohN)

expenses	*les frais* (m.) lay freh
export	*l'exportation* (f.) lehks-pohr-tah-syohN
foreign trade	*le commerce extérieur* luh koh-mehrs ehks-tay-ryuhr
goods	*les biens* (m.) lay byaN
import	*l'importation* (f.) laN-pohr-tah-syohN
interest rate	*le taux d'intérêt* luh to daN-tay-reh
invoice	*la facture* lah fahk-tewr
management	*la gestion* lah zhehs-tyohN
manager	*le (la) gérant(e)* luh (lah) zhay-rahN(t)
merchandise	*la marchandise* lah mahr-shahN-deez
money	*l'argent* (m.) lahr-zhahN
office	*le bureau* luh bew-ro
overhead expenses	*les frais généraux* (m.) lay freh zhay-nay-ro
owner	*le (la) propriétaire* luh (lah) proh-pree-ay-tehr
package	*le paquet* luh pah-keh
partner	*l'associé(e)* lah-soh-syay
payment	*le paiement* luh peh-mahN
producer	*le producteur (la productrice)* luh proh-dewk-tuhr (lah proh-dewk-trees)
property	*la propriété* lah proh-pree-ay-tay

continues

purchase	*l'achat* lah-shah
retailer	*le (la) détaillant(e)* luh (lah) day-tah-yahN(t)
sale	*la vente* lah vahNt
sample	*l'échantillon* (m.) lay-shahN-tee-yohN
selling price	*le prix de vente* luh pree duh vahNt
to send	*envoyer* ahN-vwah-yay
to send back	*renvoyer* rahN-vwah-yay
to send C.O.D. (cash on delivery)	*envoyer à livraison contre remboursement* ahN-vwah-yay ah lee-vreh-zohN kohNtr rahN-boors-mahN
to settle	*régler* ray-glay
shipment	*la cargaison* lah kahr-geh-zohN
tax	*l'impôt* (m.) laN-po
tax-exempt	*exonéré(e) d'impôts* ehgz-oh-nay-ray daN-po
trade	*le commerce* luh koh-mehrs
to transact business	*faire des affaires* fehr day zah-fehr
value-added tax	*la taxe sur la valeur ajoutée (la TVA)* lah tahks sewr lah vah-luhr ah-zhoo-tay (lah tay-vay-ah)
wholesaler	*le (la) grossiste* luh (lah) groh-seest

At the Post Office

Where's the nearest post office?	*Où est le bureau de poste le plus proche?* oo eh luh bew-ro duh pohst luh plew prohsh
Where's the nearest mailbox?	*Où est la boîte aux lettres la plus proche?* oo eh lah bwaht o lehtr lah plew prohsh
Where can I buy stamps (a phone card)?	*Où puis-je acheter des timbres (une carte téléphonique)?* oo pweezh ahsh-tay day taNbr (eewn kahrt tay-lay-foh-neek)
What's the postage rate for … ?	*Quel est l'affranchissement pour … ?* kehl eh lah-frahN-shees-mahN poor
a letter (to the United States)	*une lettre (aux États-Unis)* ewn lehtr (o zay-tah-zew-nee)
a package	*un paquet* uhN pah-keh
a postcard	*une carte postale* ewn kahrt pohs-tahl
a registered letter	*un recommandé* uhN ruh-koh-mahN-day
a special delivery	*une livraison en express* ewn lee-vreh-zohN ahN nehks-prehs
How much does this letter (this package) weigh?	*Combien pèse cette lettre (ce paquet)?* kohN-byaN pehz seht lehtr (suh pah-keh)
This package is fragile.	*Ce paquet est fragile.* suh pah-keh eh frah-zheel
When will it arrive?	*Quand arrivera-t-il (-elle)?* kahN tah-reev-rah-teel (-tehl)
Do I have to fill out a customs declaration?	*Dois-je remplir une déclaration de douane?* dwahzh rahN-pleer ewn day-klah-rah-syohN duh dwahn

Office Supplies

I need to buy …	*Je dois acheter …* zhuh dwah ahsh-tay
a ballpoint pen.	*un stylo-bille.* uhN stee-lo-bee-y
a calculator.	*une calculette.* ewn kahl-kew-leht
envelopes.	*des enveloppes.* (f.) day zahN-vlohp
an eraser.	*une gomme.* ewn gohm
glue.	*de la colle.* duh lah kohl
a notebook.	*un cahier.* uhN kah-yay
paper.	*du papier.* dew pah-pyay
paper clips.	*des trombones.* (m.) day trohN-bohn
pencils.	*des crayons.* (m.) day kreh-yohN
a pencil sharpener.	*un taille-crayon.* uhN tah-y-kreh-yohN
Post-its.	*des Post-its.* (m.) day Post-it
a ruler.	*une règle.* ewn rehgl
scotch tape.	*du Scotch.* dew skohtch
a stapler.	*une agrafeuse.* ewn ah-grah-fuhz
wrapping paper.	*du papier cadeau.* dew pah-pyay kah-do
a writing pad.	*un bloc.* uhN blohk

Faxes, Emails & Texts

Do you have a fax machine?	*Avez-vous un fax?* ah-vay-voo uhN fahks
What's your fax (cell phone) number?	*Quel est le numéro de votre fax (portable)?* kehl eh luh new-may-ro duh vohtr fahks (pohr-tahbl)
What's your email address?	*Quelle est votre adresse email?* kehl eh vohtr ah-drehs ee-mehl
I'd like to send …	*Je voudrais envoyer …* zhuh voo-dreh ahN-vwah-yay
a fax.	*un fax.* uhN fahks
an email.	*un email.* uhN nee-mehl
a text.	*un texto.* uhN tehks-to
May I send this by … ?	*Puis-je vous envoyer ceci par … ?* pweezh ahN-vwah-yay suh-see pahr
fax	*fax* fahks
email	*email* ee-mehl
text	*texto* tehks-to
Send it to me by … .	*Envoyez-le-moi par (Envoyez-la-moi par) … .* ahN-vwah-yay-luh-mwah (ahN-vwah-yay-lah-mwah pahr)
fax	*fax* fahks
email	*email* ee-mehl
text	*texto* tehks-to

continues

I didn't get your ...	*Je n'ai pas reçu votre ...* zhuh nay pah ruh-sew vohtr
fax.	*fax.* fahks
email.	*email.* ee-mehl
text.	*texto.* tehks-to
Did you receive my ... ?	*Avez-vous reçu mon ... ?* ah-vay voo ruh-sew mohN
fax	*fax* fahks
email	*email* ee-mehl
text	*texto* tehks-to

Photocopies

I'd like to make a photocopy of this document.	*Je voudrais faire une photocopie de ce document.* zhuh voo-dreh fehr ewn foh-toh-koh-pee duh suh pah-pyay (doh-kew-mahN)
I'd like to have a photocopy made.	*Je voudrais en faire faire une photocopie.* zhuh voo-dreh ahN fehr fehr ewn foh-toh-koh-pee
What's the cost per page?	*Ça coûte combien par page?* sah koot kohN-byaN pahr pahzh
Can you enlarge it (by 50 percent)?	*Pouvez-vous l'élargir (de cinquante pour cent)?* poo-vay-voo lay-lahr-zheer (duh saN-kahNt poor sahN)
Can you reduce it (by 25 percent)?	*Pouvez-vous le (la) réducir (de vingt-cinq pour cent)?* poo-vay-voo luh (lah) ray-dew-seer (duh vaN-saNk poor sahN)
Can you make a color copy?	*Pouvez-vous en faire une copie en couleurs?* poo-vay-voo ahN fehr ewn koh-pee ahN koo-luhr

Computers

I have to use a computer.	*Je dois utiliser un ordinateur.* zhuh dwah ew-tee-lee-zay uhN nohr-dee-nah-tuhr
Do you have a Mac or a PC?	*Avez-vous un Mac ou un PC?* ah-vay-voo uhN mahk ou uhN pay-say
Do you have a laptop?	*Avez-vous un ordinateur portable?* ah-vay-voo uhN nohr-dee-nah-tuhr pohr-tahbl
May I use this computer?	*Puis-je utiliser cet ordinateur?* pweezh ew-tee-lee-zay seht ohr-dee-nah-tuhr
Is it available?	*Est-il disponible?* eh-teel dee-spoh-neebl
Does it have antivirus software?	*A-t-il un logiciel antivirus?* ah-teel uhN loh-zhee-syehl ahN-tee-vee-rews
How can I connect to the internet?	*Comment puis-je me connecter à internet?* koh-mahN pweez muh koh-nehk-tay ah aN-tehr-neht
I need a wireless internet connection (Wi-Fi).	*J'ai besoin d'une connexion internet sans fil (Wi-Fi).* zhay buh-zwaN dewn koh-nehks-yohN aN-tehr-neht sahN feel (wee-fee)
Do you have wireless access?	*Avez-vous un accès sans fil?* ah-vay-voo uhN nahks-eh sahN feel
Is there (free) Wi-Fi access here?	*Il y a ici accès Wi-Fi (gratuit)?* eel yah ee-see ahks-eh wee-fee (grah-twee)
What's the Wi-Fi password?	*Quel est le mot de passe Wi-Fi?* kehl eh luh mo duh pahs wee-fee
What search engine should I use?	*Quel moteur de recherche dois-je employer?* kehl moh-tuhr duh ruh-shehrsh dwahzh ahN-plwah-yay

continues

Which websites will help me?	*Quels sites web m'aideront?* kehl seet wehb mayd-rohN
What's your email address?	*Quelle est votre adresse email?* kehl eh vohtr ah-drehs ee-mehl
What's your website?	*Quel est votre site web?* kehl eh vohtr seet wehb
Can you help me? This link isn't working.	*Pouvez-vous m'aider?* *Ce lien ne fonctionne pas.* poo-vay-voo may-day suh lyaN nuh fohnks-yohn pah
Where's the nearest internet café (hotspot)?	*Où est le cybercafé (point Wi-Fi) le plus proche?* oo eh luh see-behr-kah-fay (pwaN wee-fee) le plew prohsh
Where can I find a listing of hotspots?	*Où puis-je trouver une liste des points Wi-Fi?* oo pweezh troo-vay ewn leest day pwaN wee-fee
How can I activate (buy) an online Wi-Fi account?	*Comment puis-je activer (acheter) un compte Wi-Fi en ligne?* kohN-mahN pweezh ahk-tee-vay (ahsh-tay) uhN kohNt wee-fee ahN lee-nyuh
My computer crashed.	*Mon ordinateur a planté.* mohN nohr-dee-nah-tuhr ah plahN-tay
My computer isn't working.	*Mon ordinateur ne fonctionne pas.* mohN nohr-dee-nah-tuhr nuh fohnks-yohn pah
Where can I get it fixed?	*Où puis-je le faire réparer?* oo pweezh luh fehr ray-pah-ray
Is it possible to print this from here?	*Est-ce possible d'imprimer ceci ici?* ehs poh-seebl daN-pree-may suh-see ee-see
Please scan and send this.	*Scannez et envoyez ceci s'il vous plaît.* skah-nay ay ahN-vwah-yay suh-see seel voo pleh

The printer is running out of ink.	*L'imprimante est à court d'encre.* laN-pree-mahNt eh tah koor d'ahNkr
The printer has run out of ink.	*L'imprimante n'a plus d'encre.* laN-pree-mahNt nah plew dahNkr
Can you help me? There's a paper jam.	*Pouvez-vous m'aider?* *Il y a un bourrage papier.* poo-vay-voo may-day eel yah uhN boo-rahzh pah-pyay
Where can I print my boarding pass?	*Où puis-je imprimer ma carte d'embarquement?* oo pweezh aN-pree-may mah kahrt dahN-bahrk-mahN

Computer Words & Expressions

access	*l'accès* (m.) lahks-eh
antivirus software	*le logiciel antivirus* luh loh-zhee-syehl ahN-tee-vee-rews
app	*l'appli(cation)* (f.) lah-plee(kah-syohN)
to attach	*attacher* ah-tah-shay
attachment	*la pièce jointe* lah pyehs zhwaNt
backup	*la sauvegarde* lah sov-gahrd
blog	*le blog(ue)* luh blohg
bookmark	*le signet* luh see-nyeh
to bookmark	*ajouter à ses favoris* ah-zhoo-tay ah say fah-voh-ree
to boot up	*démarrer* day-mah-ray
browser	*le navigateur* luh nah-vee-gah-tuhr

continues

cartridge	*la cartouche* lah kahr-toosh
to click	*cliquer* klee-kay
clipboard	*le presse-papier* luh prehs-pah-pyay
computer	*l'ordinateur* (m.) lohr-dee-nah-tuhr
computer science	*l'informatique* (f.) laN-fohr-mah-teek
to copy	*copier* koh-pyay
connection	*la connexion* lah koh-nehks-yohN
cursor	*le curseur* luh kewr-suhr
to cut	*couper* koo-pay
desktop	*le bureau* luh bew-ro
database	*la base de données* lah bahz duh doh-nay
to delete	*supprimer* sew-pree-may
dictionary	*le dictionnaire* luh deek-syoh-nehr
document	*le document* luh doh-kew-mahN
to download	*télécharger* tay-lay-shahr-zhay
to drag	*traîner* tray-nay
email	*le email* luh ee-mehl
file	*le fichier* luh feesh-yay
firewall	*le pare-feu* luh pahr-fuh
folder	*le dossier* luh do-syay

function key	*la touche de fonction* lah toosh duh fohnks-yohN
graphics	*les graphismes* (m.) lay grah-feez-muh
hacker	*le hackeur (la hackeuse)* luh ahk-uhr (lah ahk-uhz)
home page	*la page d'accueil* lah pahzh dah-kuh-y
icon	*l'icône* (f.) lee-kon
ink	*l'encre* (f.) lahNkr
to insert	*insérer* aN-say-ray
internet café	*le cybercafé* luh see-behr-kah-fay
junk mail (spam)	*le courrier indésirable (le pourriel)* luh koo-ryay aN-day-zee-rahbl (luh poo-ryhl)
key	*la touche* lah toosh
keyboard	*le clavier* luh klah-vyay
laptop computer	*l'ordinateur portable* (m.) lohr-dee-nah-tuhr pohr-tahbl
line	*la ligne* lah lee-nyuh
link	*le lien* luh lyaN
memory	*la mémoire* lah may-mwahr
to merge	*fusionner* few-syoh-nay
message	*le message* luh meh-sahzh
modem	*le modem* luh moh-dehm
monitor	*le moniteur* luh moh-nee-tuhr

continues

mouse	*la souris* lah soo-ree
network	*le réseau* luh ray-zo
password	*le mot de passe* luh mo duh pahs
to paste	*coller* koh-lay
portal	*le portail* luh pohr-tah-y
to print	*imprimer* aN-pree-may
printer	*l'imprimante* (f.) laN-pree-mahNt
program	*le programme* luh proh-grahm
public domain	*le domaine public* luh doh-mehn pew-bleek
to reboot	*redémarrer* ruh-day-mah-ray
to save	*enregistrer* ahN-ruh-zhee-stray
to scan	*scanner (numériser)* skah-nay (new-may-ree-zay)
screen	*l'écran* (m.) lay-krahN
search engine	*le moteur de recherche* luh moh-tuhr duh ruh-shehrsh
server	*le serveur* luh sehr-vuhr
shortcut (keyboard)	*le raccourci* luh rah-koor-see
site	*le site* luh seet
software	*le logiciel* luh loh-zhee-syehl
spam	*le spam* luh spahm
spell-checker	*le correcteur d'orthographe* luh koh-rehk-tuhr dohr-toh-grahf

spreadsheet	*la feuille de calcul* lah fuh-y duh kahl-kewl
symbol	*le symbole* luh saN-bohl
thesaurus	*le dictionnaire des synonymes* luh deek-syoh-nehr day see-noh-neem
thread	*le fil* luh feel
thumb (USB) drive	*la clé USB* lah klay ew-ehs-bay
touchscreen	*l'écran tactile* (m.) lay-krahN tahk-teel
to turn off	*éteindre* ay-taNdr
to turn on	*allumer* ah-lew-may
tweet	*le tweet* luh tweet
window	*la fenêtre* lah fuh-nehtr
word processor	*le traitement de texte* luh treht-mahN duh tehkst
Zoom meeting	*la réunion de Zoom* lah ray-ew-nyohN duh Zoom

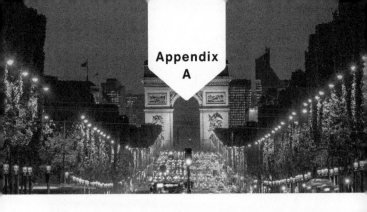

English to French Dictionary

a, an	*un, une* uhN, ewn
able (to be able)	*pouvoir* poo-vwahr
about	*de environ* duh ahN-vee-rohN
above	*au-dessus de* o duh-sew duh
to accompany	*accompagner* ah-koh-pah-nyay
address	*adresse* (f.) ah-drehs
to adjust	*régler* ray-glay
after	*après* ah-preh
afternoon	*après-midi* (m.) ah-preh-mee-dee
again	*encore une fois* ahN-kohr ewn fwah
against	*contre* kohNtr
ago (+ time)	*il y a* eel yah
air conditioning	*climatisation* (f.) klee-mah-tee-zah-syohN
airline	*ligne aérienne* (f.) lee-nyuh ah-ay-ryan
airport	*aéroport* (m.) ah-ay-roh-pohr
all	*tout(e)(s)* too(t)
allergic	*allergique* ah-lehr-zheek
almost	*presque* prehsk
already	*déjà* day-zhah
also	*aussi* o-see

always	*toujours* too-zhoor
American consulate	*consulat américain* (m.) kohN-sew-lah ah-may-ree-kaN
American embassy	*ambassade américaine* (f.) ahN-bah-sahd ah-may-ree-kehn
among	*parmi* pahr-mee
another	*un(e) autre* uhN (ewn) otr
apple	*pomme* (f.) pohm
appointment	*rendez-vous* (m.) rahN-day-voo
April	*avril* (m.) ah-vreel
arm	*bras* (m.) brah
around (surrounding)	*autour de* o-toor duh
to arrive	*arriver* ah-ree-vay
ashtray	*cendrier* (m.) sahN-dree-yay
to ask	*demander* duh-mahN-day
aspirins	*aspirines* (f.) ahs-pee-reen
at	*à* ah (o, ah lah, ahl, o)
ATM	*distributeur* (m.) dees-tree-bew-tuhr
August	*août* (m.) oo, oot
autumn	*automne* (m.) o-tohn
available	*disponible* dees-poh-neebl
bad	*mal, mauvais(e)* mahl, mo-veh(z)

bag	*sac* (m.) sahk
bakery	*boulangerie* (f.) boo-lahN-zhree
ballpoint pen	*stylo-bille* (m.) stee-lo-bee-y
banana	*banane* (f.) bah-nahn
Band-Aid	*pansement adhésif* (m.) pahNs-mahN ahd-ay-zeef
bandage	*pansement* (m.) pahNs-mahN
bank	*banque* (f.) bahNk
bathing suit	*maillot de bain* (m.) mah-yo duh baN
bathroom	*salle* [f.] *de bains, toilettes* (f.) sahl duh baN, twah-leht
to be	*être* ehtr
beach	*plage* (f.) plahzh
because	*parce que* pahrs-kuh
beef	*bœuf* (m.) buhf
beer	*bière* (f.) byehr
before	*avant de* ah-vahN duh
to begin	*commencer* koh-mahN-say
behind	*derrière* dehr-yehr
bellhop	*chasseur* (m.) shah-suhr
below, beneath	*au-dessous de* o duh-soo duh
between	*entre* ahNtr

big	*grand(e)* grahN(d)
bill (commerce)	*facture* (f.), *note* (f.) fahk-tewr, noht
bill (money)	*billet* (m.) bee-yeh
bill (restaurant)	*addition* (f.) ah-dee-syohN
black	*noir(e)* nwahr
blanket	*couverture* (f.) koo-vehr-tewr
block (street)	*pâté* [m.] *de maison* pah-tay duh meh-zohN
blouse	*chemisier* (m.) shuh-mee-zyay
blue	*bleu(e)* bluh
to board	*embarquer* ahN-bahr-kay
boarding pass	*carte* [f.] *d'embarquement* kahrt dahN-bahrk-mahN
boat	*bateau* (m.) bah-to
book	*livre* (m.) leevr
bookstore	*librairie* (f.) lee-breh-ree
boots	*bottes* (f.) boht
to borrow	*emprunter* ahN-pruhN-tay
bottle	*bouteille* (f.) boo-teh-y
bottle (baby)	*biberon* (m.) bee-brohN
box	*boîte* (f.) bwaht
brand name	*marque* (f.) mahrk

bread	*pain* (m.) paN
to bring (things)	*apporter* ah-pohr-tay
brother	*frère* (m.) frehr
brown	*brun(e)*, *marron* bruhN (brewn), mah-rohN
bus	*autobus* (m.), *bus* (m.) o-toh-bews, bews
bus stop	*arrêt d'autobus* (m.) ah-reh do-toh-bews
business card	*carte* [f.] *de visite* kahrt duh vee-zeet
butcher shop	*boucherie* (f.) boosh-ree
butter	*beurre* (m.) buhr
to buy	*acheter* ahsh-tay
by	*par* pahr
cake	*gâteau* (m.) gah-to
calculator	*calculette* (f.) kahl-kew-leht
to call	*appeler* ah-play
can	*boîte* (f.) bwaht
can (to be able to)	*pouvoir* poo-vwahr
candy	*bonbons* (m.) bohN-bohN
candy store	*confiserie* (f.) kohN-feez-ree
car	*voiture* (f.), *auto* (f.) vwah-tewr, o-to
cash	*espèces* (f.), *argent liquide* (m.) ehs-pehs, ahr-zhahN lee-keed

cash advance	*avance* [f.] *de fonds* ah-vahNs duh fohN
to cash (a check)	*toucher (un chèque)* too-shay (uhN shehk)
cashier	*caissier (caissière)* keh-syay (keh-syehr)
cat	*chat* (m.) shah
cell phone	*portable* (m.), *mobile* (m.), *cellulaire* (m.) pohr-tahbl, moh-beel, seh-lew-lehr
chair	*chaise* (f.) shehz
change (coins)	*monnaie* (f.) moh-neh
to change	*échanger, changer* ay-shahN-zhay, shahN-zhay
check (money)	*chèque* (m.) shehk
cheese	*fromage* (m.) froh-mahzh
cherry	*cerise* (f.) suh-reez
chicken	*poulet* (m.) poo-leh
church	*église* (f.) ay-gleez
clean	*propre* prohpr
clock	*horloge* (f.) ohr-lohzh
to close	*fermer* fehr-may
clothing store	*magasin* [m.] *de vêtements* mah-gah-zaN duh veht-mahN
coffee	*café* (m.) kah-fay
cold, to be cold (person)	*avoir froid* ah-vwahr frwah

cold, to be cold (weather)	*faire froid* fehr frwah
cold (illness)	*rhume* (m.) rewm
color	*couleur* (f.) koo-luhr
to come	*venir* vuh-neer
computer	*ordinateur* (m.) ohr-dee-nah-tuhr
cookie	*biscuit* (m.) bees-kwee
to cost	*coûter* koo-tay
country	*pays* (m.) pay-ee
credit card	*carte* [f.] *de crédit* kahrt duh kray-dee
crib	*berceau* (m.) behr-so
cup	*tasse* (f.) tahs
(border) customs	*douane* (f.) dwahn
dark (color)	*foncé(e)* fohN-say
data	*données* (f.) doh-nay
date	*date* (f.) daht
daughter	*fille* (f.) fee-y
day, daytime	*jour* (m.), *journée* (f.) zhoor, zhoor-nay
debit card	*carte* [f.] *de débit* kahrt duh day-bee
decaffeinated	*décaféiné(e)* day-kah-fay-ee-nay
December	*décembre* (m.) day-sahNbr

to decide	*décider* day-see-day
to declare	*déclarer* day-klah-ray
to deliver	*livrer* lee-vray
dentist	*dentiste* (m./f.) dahN-teest
deodorant	*déodorant* (m.) day-oh-doh-rahN
department store	*grand magasin* (m.) grahN mah-gah-zaN
departure	*départ* (m.) day-pahr
to describe	*décrire* day-kreer
to desire	*désirer* day-zee-ray
dessert	*dessert* (m.) day-sehr
dictionary	*dictionnaire* (m.) deek-syoh-nehr
difficult	*difficile* dee-fee-seel
dirty	*sale* sahl
disability access	*accès* [m.] *pour les personnes* *handicapées* ahks-eh poor lay pehr-sohn ahN-dee-kah-pay
disability services	*services* [m. pl.] *pour* *les personnes handicapées* sehr-vees poor lay pehr-sohn ahN-dee-kah-pay
disabled	*handicapé(e)* ahN-dee-kah-pay
discount	*remise* (f.), *réduction* (f.) ruh-meez, ray-dewk-syohN
to do	*faire* fehr

doctor	*médecin, docteur(e)* mayd-saN, dohk-tuhr
dog	*chien* (m.) shyaN
door	*porte* (f.) pohrt
downtown	*centre-ville* (m.) sahNtr-veel
dozen	*douzaine* (f.) doo-zehn
dress	*robe* (f.) rohb
to drink	*boire* bwahr
during	*pendant* pahN-dahN
each	*chaque* shahk
ear	*oreille* (f.) oh-reh-y
early	*tôt* to
to earn	*gagner* gah-nyay
east	*est* (m.) ehst
easy	*facile* fah-seel
to eat	*manger* mahN-zhay
egg	*œuf* (m.) uhf
eight	*huit* weet
eighteen	*dix-huit* dee-zweet
eighty	*quatre-vingts* kahtr-vaN
electricity	*électricité* (f.) ay-lehk-tree-see-tay

elevator	*ascenseur* (m.) ah-sahN-suhr
eleven	*onze* ohNz
email	*email* ee-mehl
employee	*employé(e)* ahN-plwah-yay
to end	*terminer, finir* tehr-mee-nay, fee-neer
English (language)	*anglais* (m.) ahN-gleh
English (nationality)	*anglais(e)* ahN-gleh(z)
to enjoy	*jouir de* zhoo-eer duh
enough (of)	*assez de* ah-say duh
entertainment guide	*programme* [m.] *des spectacles* proh-grahm day spehk-tahkl
entrance	*entrée* (f.) ahN-tray
evening	*soir* (m.) swahr
to exchange	*échanger* ay-shahN-zhay
exchange rate	*taux* [m.] *de change* to duh shahNzh
excuse me	*pardon (excusez-moi)* pahr-dohN (ehks-kew-zay-mwah)
exit	*sortie* (f.) sohr-tee
to explain	*expliquer* ehks-plee-kay
eye	*œil* (sing.), *yeux* (pl.) uh-y, yuh
facing	*en face de, face à* ahN fahs duh, fahs ah
family	*famille* (f.) fah-mee-y

far (from)	*loin (de)* lwaN (duh)
fare	*tarif* (m.) tah-reef
father	*père* (m.) pehr
February	*février* (m.) fay-vree-yay
fifteen	*quinze* kaNz
fifty	*cinquante* saN-kahNt
to find	*trouver* troo-vay
first	*premier (première)* pruh-myay (pruh-myehr)
fish	*poisson* (m.) pwah-sohN
fish store	*poissonerie* (f.) pwah-sohn-ree
fitness center	*salle* [f.] *de gym* sahl duh zheem
five	*cinq* saNk
to fix	*réparer* ray-pah-ray
flight	*vol* (m.) vohl
floor (story)	*étage* (m.) ay-tahzh
to follow	*suivre* sweevr
food	*nourriture* (f.) noo-ree-tewr
foot	*pied* (m.) pyay
for	*pour* poor
fork	*fourchette* (f.) foor-sheht

forty	*quarante* kah-rahNt
four	*quatre* kahtr
fourteen	*quatorze* kah-tohrz
French (language)	*français* (m.) frahN-seh
French (nationality)	*français(e)* frahN-seh(z)
Friday	*vendredi* (m.) vahN-druh-dee
from	*de* duh
front, in front (of)	*devant* duh-vahN
gasoline	*essence* (f.) eh-sahNs
gate (airport)	*porte* (f.) pohrt
gift shop	*boutique* [f.] *de cadeaux* boo-teek duh kah-do
to give	*donner* doh-nay
glass	*verre* (m.) vehr
glove	*gant* (m.) gahN
to go	*aller* ah-lay
to go out	*sortir* sohr-teer
gold	*or* (m.) ohr
good	*bon(ne)* bohN (bohn)
goodbye	*au revoir* o ruh-vwahr
gray	*gris(e)* gree(z)

green	*vert(e)* vehr(t)
grocery store	*épicerie* (f.) ay-pees-ree
ground floor	*rez-de-chaussée* (m.) rayd sho-say
guidebook	*guide* (m.) geed
hair	*cheveux* (m.) shuh-vuh
half	*demi(e), moitié* duh-mee, mwah-tyay
ham	*jambon* (m.) zhahN-bohN
hamburger	*hamburger* (m.) ahm-boor-guhr
hand	*main* (f.) maN
hanger	*cintre* (m.) saNtr
happy	*heureux (heureuse), content(e)* uh-ruh (uh-ruhz), kohN-tahN(t)
hat	*chapeau* (m.) shah-po
to have	*avoir* ah-vwahr
to have an ache (in)	*avoir mal à* ah-vwahr mahl ah
to have to	*devoir* duh-vwahr
he	*il* eel
head	*tête* (f.) teht
to hear	*entendre* ahN-tahNdr
heart	*cœur* (m.) kuhr

hello	*bonjour* (general), *allô* (on the phone) bohN-zhoor, ah-lo
to help	*aider* ay-day
here	*ici* ee-see
holiday	*fête* (f.) feht
to hope	*espérer* ehs-pay-ray
hospital	*hôpital* (m.) o-pee-tahl
hot, to be hot (person)	*avoir chaud* ah-vwahr sho
hot, to be hot (weather)	*faire chaud* fehr sho
hour	*heure* (f.) uhr
house	*maison* (f.) meh-zohN
housekeeping service	*entretien* (m.) ahNtr-tyaN
how	*comment* koh-mahN
how much, many	*combien* kohN-byaN
hundred	*cent* sahN
hungry, to be hungry	*avoir faim* ah-vwahr faN
hurry, to be in a hurry	*avoir hâte (de)* ah-vwahr aht (duh)
husband	*mari* (m.) mah-ree
I	*je* zhuh
ice cream	*glace* (f.) glahs

ice cubes	*glaçons* (m. pl.) glah-sohN
in	*dans, en* dahN, ahN
included	*compris(e)* kohN-pree(z)
information	*renseignements* (m.) rahN-seh-nyuh-mahN
inside	*dedans* duh-dahN
instead of	*au lieu de* o lyuh duh
interpreter	*interprète* (m./f.) aN-tehr-preht
jacket	*veste* (f.) vehst
January	*janvier* (m.) zhahN-vyay
jar	*pot* (m.) po
jelly	*confiture* (f.) kohN-fee-tewr
jewelry store	*bijouterie* (f.) bee-zhoo-tree
juice	*jus* (m.) zhew
July	*juillet* (m.) zhwee-yeh
June	*juin* (m.) zhwaN
to keep	*garder* gahr-day
ketchup	*ketchup* (m.) keht-chuhp
key	*clé* (f.) klay
kitchen	*cuisine* (f.) kwee-zeen
knife	*couteau* (m.) koo-to

lamb	*agneau* (m.) ah-nyo
lamp	*lampe* (f.) lahNp
to land	*atterrir* ah-tay-reer
laptop (wireless)	*ordinateur portable* [m.] *(sans fil)* ohr-dee-nah-tuhr pohr-tahbl (sahN feel)
last	*dernier (dernière)* dehr-nyay (dehr-nyehr)
to last	*durer* dew-ray
late (in the day)	*tard* tahr
late (in arriving)	*en retard* ahN ruh-tahr
to learn	*apprendre* ah-prahNdr
leather	*cuir* (m.) kweer
to leave	*quitter, partir* kee-tay, pahr-teer
left (direction)	*gauche* gosh
leg	*jambe* (f.) zhahNb
lemon	*citron* (m.) see-trohN
to lend	*prêter* pray-tay
less	*moins* mwaN
letter	*lettre* (f.) lehtr
lettuce	*laitue* (f.) lay-tew
library	*bibliothèque* (f.) bee-blee-oh-tehk

light (color)	*clair(e)* klehr
light (weight)	*léger (légère)* lay-zhay (lay-zhehr)
to like	*aimer* ay-may
liquor store	*magasin* [m.] *de vins* *et spiritueux* mah-gah-zaN duh vaN ay spee-ree-tew-uh
to listen to	*écouter* ay-koo-tay
(a) little	*(un) peu* (uhN) puh
to live	*vivre* (general), *habiter* (to reside) veevr, ah-bee-tay
long	*long(ue)* lohN(g)
to look at	*regarder* ruh-gahr-day
to look for	*chercher* shehr-shay
to lose	*perdre* pehrdr
lucky, to be lucky	*avoir de la chance* ah-vwahr duh lah shahNs
magazine	*revue* (f.) ruh-vew
mailbox	*boîte* [f.] *aux lettres* bwaht o lehtr
to make	*faire* fehr
makeup	*maquillage* (m.) mah-kee-yahzh
mall	*centre commercial* (m.) sahNtr koh-mehr-syahl
manager	*gérant(e)* zhay-rahN(t)

map	*carte* (f.) kahrt
March	*mars* (m.) mahrs
market	*marché* (m.) mahr-shay
married	*marié(e)* mah-ryay
match (fire)	*allumette* (f.) ah-lew-meht
May	*mai* (m.) meh
mayonnaise	*mayonnaise* (f.) mah-yoh-nehz
to mean	*signifier, vouloir dire* see-nee-fyay, voo-lwahr deer
meat	*viande* (f.) vyahNd
medicine	*médicament* (m.) may-dee-kah-mahN
meeting	*rendez-vous* (m.) rahN-day-voo
menu	*menu* (m.), *carte* (f.) muh-new, kahrt
message	*message* (m.) meh-sahzh
midnight	*minuit* (m.) mee-nwee
milk	*lait* (m.) leh
mineral water	*eau minérale* (f.) o mee-nay-rahl
minute	*minute* (f.) mee-newt
mirror	*miroir* (m.) mee-rwahr
Monday	*lundi* (m.) luhN-dee
money	*argent* (m.) ahr-zhahN

money exchange	*bureau* [m.] *de change* bew-ro duh shahNzh
month	*mois* (m.) mwah
monument	*monument* (m.) moh-new-mahN
more	*plus* plew
morning	*matin* (m.) mah-taN
mother	*mère* (f.) mehr
mouth	*bouche* (f.) boosh
mouthwash	*bain* [m.] *de bouche* baN duh boosh
movie	*film* (m.) feelm
movies, movie theater	*cinéma* (m.) see-nay-mah
museum	*musée* (m.) mew-zay
mushroom	*champignon* (m.) shahN-pee-nyohN
mustard	*moutarde* (f.) moo-tahrd
napkin	*serviette* (f.) sehr-vyeht
narrow	*étroit(e)* ay-trwah(t)
near (to)	*près de* preh duh
necessary	*nécessaire* nay-say-sehr
to need	*avoir besoin de* ah-vwahr buh-zwaN duh
new	*nouveau (nouvelle)* noo-vo (noo-vehl)
news	*informations* (f. pl.) aN-fohr-mah-syohN

newspaper	*journal* (m.) zhoor-nahl
newsstand	*kiosk à journaux* (m.) kee-ohsk ah zhoor-no
next	*prochain(e)* proh-shaN (proh-shehn)
next to	*à côté de* ah ko-tay
nice	*sympathique* saN-pah-teek
nine	*neuf* nuf
nineteen	*dix-neuf* deez-nuhf
ninety	*quatre-vingt-dix* kahtr-vaN-dees
noon	*midi* (m.) mee-dee
north	*nord* (m.) nohr
November	*novembre* (m.) noh-vahNbr
now	*maintenant* maNt-nahN
number	*numéro* (m.) new-may-ro
ocean	*océan* (m.) oh-say-ahN
October	*octobre* (m.) ohk-tohbr
of	*de* duh
of course	*bien sûr* byaN sewr
office	*bureau* (m.) bew-ro
office (medical)	*cabinet* (m.) kah-bee-neh
often	*souvent* soo-vahN

old	*vieux* (m.), *vieil* [(m.) before vowel sound], *vieille* (f.) vyuh, vyay, vyay
on	*sur* sewr
one	*un(e)* uhN (ewn)
onion	*oignon* (m.) oh-nyohN
to open	*ouvrir* oo-vreer
opposite	*en face* ahN fahs
orange (color)	*orange* oh-rahNzh
orange (fruit)	*orange* (f.) oh-rahNzh
to order	*commander* koh-mahN-day
outside	*dehors* duh-ohr
package	*paquet* (m.) pah-keh
pain	*douleur* (f.), *mal* doo-luhr, mahl
pants	*pantalon* (m.) pahN-tah-lohN
paper	*papier* (m.) pah-pyay
parent	*parent* (m.) pah-rahN
park	*parc* (m.) pahrk
to participate	*participer* pahr-tee-see-pay
passport	*passeport* (m.) pahs-pohr
password	*mot de passe* (m.) mo duh pahs

to pay	*payer* pay-ay
pencil	*crayon* (m.) kreh-yohN
pepper (seasoning)	*poivre* (m.) pwahvr
pharmacy	*pharmacie* (f.) fahr-mah-see
to phone	*téléphoner* tay-lay-foh-nay
phone book	*annuaire* [m.] *téléphonique* ah-new-ehr tay-lay-foh-neek
phone card	*carte téléphonique* (f.) kahrt tay-lay-foh-neek
photocopy	*photocopie* (f.) foh-toh-koh-pee
phone number	*numéro* [m.] *de téléphone* new-may-ro duh tay-lay-fohn
pill	*pilule* (f.) pee-lewl
pillow	*oreiller* (m.) oh-reh-yay
pink	*rose* roz
place	*lieu* (m.) lyuh
plane	*avion* (m.) ah-vyohN
plate	*assiette* (f.) ah-syeht
to play	*jouer* zoo-ay
please	*s'il vous plaît* seel voo pleh
pocketbook	*sac* (m.) sahk
police officer	*agent(e) de police* ah-zhahN(t) duh poh-lees
police station	*commissariat* [m.] *de police* koh-mee-sah-ryah duh poh-lees

pool (swimming)	*piscine* (f.) pee-seen
poor	*pauvre* povr
postage	*affranchissement* (m.) ah-frahN-shees-mahN
postcard	*carte postale* (f.) kahrt pohs-tahl
potato	*pomme de terre* (f.) pohm duh tehr
to prefer	*préférer* pray-fay-ray
prescription	*ordonnance* (f.) ohr-doh-nahNs
pretty	*joli(e)* zhoh-lee
price	*prix* (m.) pree
problem	*problème* (m.) proh-blehm
to purchase	*acheter* ahsh-tay
purple	*pourpre* poor-pr
to put	*mettre* mehtr
quarter	*quart* (m.) kahr
question	*question* (f.) kehs-tyohN
quickly	*vite* veet
to read	*lire* leer
receipt	*reçu* (m.) ruh-sew
to receive	*recevoir* ruh-suh-vwahr
to recommend	*recommander, conseiller* ruh-koh-mahN-day, kohN-say-yay

red	*rouge* roozh
refund	*remboursement* (m.) rahN-boors-mahN
to remember	*rappeler* rah-play
to rent	*louer* loo-ay
to repair	*réparer* ray-pah-ray
restaurant	*restaurant* (m.) reh-stoh-rahN
retired	*en retraite* ahN ruh-treht
to return (go back)	*rentrer, retourner* rahN-tray, ruh-toor-nay
to return (item)	*rendre* rahNdr
rice	*riz* (m.) ree
rideshare	*covoiturage* (m.) ko-vwah-tew-rahzh
right (direction)	*droit(e)* drwah(t)
room	*chambre* (f.), *salle* (f.) shahNbr, sahl
safe	*coffre-fort* (m.) kohfr-fohr
salad	*salade* (f.) sah-lahd
sale (bargain)	*bonne affaire* (f.) bohn ah-fehr
salesperson	*vendeur (vendeuse)* vahN-duhr (vahN-duhz)
salt	*sel* (m.) sehl
sample	*échantillon* (m.) ay-shahN-tee-yohN
Saturday	*samedi* (m.) sahm-dee

sauce	*sauce* (f.) sos
saucer	*soucoupe* (f.) soo-koop
to say	*dire* deer
scissors	*ciseaux* (m.) see-zo
sea	*mer* (f.) mehr
seafood	*fruits* [m. pl.] *de mer* frwee duh mehr
seat	*place* (f.) plahs
seat belt	*ceinture* [f.] *de sécurité* saN-tewr duh say-kew-ree-tay
to see	*voir* vwahr
self-employed	*indépendant(e)* aN-day-pahN-dahn(t)
to sell	*vendre* vahNdr
to send	*envoyer* ahN-vwah-yay
September	*septembre* (m.) sehp-tahNbr
seven	*sept* seht
seventeen	*dix-sept* dee-seht
seventy	*soixante-dix* swah-sahNt-dees
shampoo	*shampooing* (m.) shahN-pwaN
she	*elle* ehl
shellfish	*crustacés* (m. pl.) kroo-stah-say
shirt	*chemise* (f.) shuh-meez

shoe	*soulier* (m.), *chaussure* (f.) soo-lyay, sho-sewr
shoe store	*magasin* [m.] *de chaussures* mah-gah-zaN duh sho-sewr
short	*court(e)* koor(t)
show	*spectacle* (m.) spehk-tahkl
to show	*montrer* mohN-tray
sick	*malade* mah-lahd
to sign	*signer* see-nyay
silk	*soie* (f.) swah
silver	*argent* (m.) ahr-zhahN
since (time)	*depuis* duh-pwee
single (unmarried)	*célibataire* say-lee-bah-tehr
sister	*sœur* (f.) suhr
six	*six* sees
sixteen	*seize* sehz
sixty	*soixante* swah-sahNt
skirt	*jupe* (f.) zhoop
slowly	*lentement* lahNt-mahN
small	*petit(e)* puh-tee(t)
to smoke	*fumer* few-may
sneakers	*baskets* (f. pl.), *tennis* (m. pl.) bahs-keht, tay-nees

sock	*chaussette* (f.) sho-seht
soda	*soda* (m.) soh-dah
son	*fils* (m.) fees
soon	*bientôt* byaN-to
(I'm) sorry	*désolé(e)* day-zoh-lay
soup	*soupe* (f.) soop
south	*sud* (m.) sewd
souvenir store	*magasin* [m.] *de souvenirs* mah-gah-zaN duh soov-neer
to speak	*parler* pahr-lay
to spend (money)	*dépenser* day-pahN-say
to spend (time)	*passer* pah-say
spicy	*épicé(e)* ay-pee-say
spoon	*cuillère* (f.) kwee-yehr
spring	*printemps* (m.) praN-tahN
stadium	*stade* (m.) stahd
stamp (mail)	*timbre* (m.) taNbr
still (up to now)	*toujours* too-zhoor
stomach	*estomac* (m.), *ventre* (m.) ehs-toh-mah, vahNtr
stone	*pierre* (f.) pyehr
stopover	*escale* (f.) eh-skahl

store	*magasin* (m.), *boutique* (f.) mah-gah-zaN, boo-teek
strawberry	*fraise* (f.) frehz
street	*rue* (f.) rew
subway	*métro* (m.) may-tro
subway station	*station de métro* (f.) stah-syohN duh may-tro
sugar	*sucre* (m.) sewkr
suitcase	*valise* (f.) vah-leez
summer	*été* (m.) ay-tay
Sunday	*dimanche* (m.) dee-mahNsh
(sun)glasses	*lunettes* [f. pl.] *(de soleil)* lew-neht (duh soh-leh-y)
supermarket	*supermarché* (m.) sew-pehr-mahr-shay
sweater	*pull* (m.) pewl
sweet	*doux (douce)* doo(s)
table	*table* (f.) tahbl
to take	*prendre* prahNdr
to take place	*avoir lieu* ah-vwahr lyuh
to talk	*parler* pahr-lay
tall	*grand(e)* grahN(d)
tax	*impôt* (m.), *taxe* (f.) aN-po, tahks
taxi	*taxi* (m.) tahks-ee

taxi stand	*station* [m.] *de taxis* stah-syohN duh tahks-ee
tea	*thé* (m.) tay
teaspoon	*petite cuillère* (f.) puh-teet kwee-yehr
T-shirt	*tee-shirt* (m.) tee-shehrt
telephone	*téléphone* (m.) tay-lay-fohn
to telephone	*téléphoner* tay-lay-foh-nay
television	*télévision* (f.) tay-lay-vee-zyohN
to tell	*dire* deer
ten	*dix* dees
thank you	*merci* mehr-see
theater	*théâtre* (m.) tay-ahtr
then	*puis, alors* pwee, ah-lohr
there is (are)	*il y a* eel yah
they	*ils, elles* eel, ehl
thirteen	*treize* trehz
thirty	*trente* trahNt
thousand	*mille* meel
three	*trois* trwah
throat	*gorge* (f.) gohrzh
through (by)	*par* pahr

Thursday	*jeudi* (m.) zhuh-dee
ticket	*billet* (m.), *ticket* (m.) bee-yeh, tee-kay
time	*temps* (m.) (general), *heure* (f.) (by the clock) tahN, uhr
on time	*à l'heure* ah luhr
tip (gratuity)	*pourboire* (m.) poor-bwahr
tissue	*mouchoir* [m.] *en papier* moo-shwahr ahN pah-pyay
to	*à* ah
tobacco store	*bureau* [m.] *de tabac* bew-ro duh tah-bah
today	*aujourd'hui* o-zhoor-dwee
tomato	*tomate* (f.) toh-maht
tomorrow	*demain* duh-maN
too (also)	*aussi* o-see
too much	*trop* tro
tooth	*dent* (f.) dahN
toothbrush	*brosse* [f.] *à dents* brohs ah dahN
toothpaste	*pâte* [f.] *dentifrice* paht dahN-tee-frees
towel	*serviette* (f.) sehr-vyeht
train	*train* (m.) traN
train station	*gare* (f.) gahr

to travel	*voyager* vwah-yah-zhay
trip	*voyage* (m.) vwah-yahzh
to try, to try on	*essayer* ay-say-yay
Tuesday	*mardi* (m.) mahr-dee
turkey	*dinde* (f.) daNd
twelve	*douze* dooz
twenty	*vingt* vaN
two	*deux* duh
umbrella	*parapluie* (m.) pah-rah-plwee
under	*sous, dessous* soo, duh-soo
to understand	*comprendre* kohN-prahNdr
United States	*États-Unis* (m. pl.) ay-tah-zew-nee
until	*jusqu'à* zhews-kah
upon	*sur* sewr
us	*nous* noo
to use	*utiliser, employer* oo-tee-lee-zay, ahN-plwah-yay
vegan	*végétalien(ne)* vay-zhay-tah-lyaN (-lyehn)
vegetable	*légume* (m.) lay-gewm
vegetarian	*végétarien(ne)* vay-zhay-tah-ryaN (-ryehn)
very	*très* treh

to visit (person)	*rendre visite à* rahNdr vee-zeet ah
to visit (place)	*visiter* vee-zee-tay
to wait for	*attendre* ah-tahNdr
wallet	*portefeuille* (m.) pohr-tuh-fuh-y
to want	*vouloir* voo-lwahr
watch	*montre* (f.) mohNtr
to watch	*regarder* ruh-gahr-day
water	*eau* (f.) o
we	*nous* noo
weather	*temps* (m.) tahN
weather forecast	*météo* (f.) may-tay-o
Wednesday	*mercredi* (m.) mehr-kruh-dee
week	*semaine* (f.) suh-mehn
welcome	*bienvenue* byaN-vuh-new
well	*bien* byaN
west	*ouest* (m.) wehst
what	*que, quoi* kuh, kwah
when	*quand* kahN
where	*où* oo
which	*quel(le)* kehl

white	*blanc(he)* blahN (blahNsh)
who(m)	*qui* kee
why	*pourquoi* poor-kwah
wide	*large* lahrzh
widow(er)	*veuve (veuf)* vuhv (vuhf)
wife	*femme* (f.) fahm
window (building)	*fenêtre* fuh-nehtr
window (car)	*vitre* (f.) veetr
wine	*vin* (m.) vaN
winter	*hiver* (m.) ee-vehr
without	*sans* sahN
wool	*laine* (f.) lehn
to work (employment)	*travailler* trah-vah-yay
to work (function)	*fonctionner* fohnk-syoh-nay
to write	*écrire* ay-kreer
yellow	*jaune* zhon
yesterday	*hier* yehr
you	*tu, vous* tew, voo
you're welcome	*de rien, pas de quoi* duh ryaN, pah duh kwah
young	*jeune* zhuhn

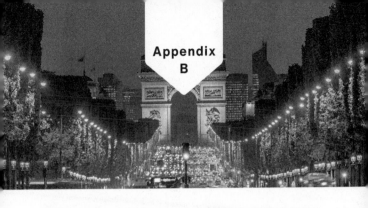

French to English Dictionary

à ah	at, to
à côté de ah ko-tay duh	next to
à l'heure ah luhr	on time
accompagner ah-koh-pah-nyay	to accompany
acheter ahsh-tay	to buy, purchase
addition (f.) ah-dee-syohN	bill (restaurant)
aéroport (m.) ah-ay-roh-pohr	airport
affranchissement (m.) ah-frahN-shees-mahN	postage
agneau (m.) ah-nyo	lamb
aider ay-day	to help
aimer ay-may	to like
aller ah-lay	to go
allergique ah-lehr-zheek	allergic
allô ah-lo	hello (on the phone)
allumette (f.) ah-lew-meht	match (fire)
alors ah-lohr	then
ambassade américaine (f.) ahN-bah-sahd ah-may-ree-kehn	American embassy
anglais (m.) ahN-gleh	English (language)
anglais(e) ahN-gleh(z)	English (nationality)
annuaire téléphonique (m.) ah-new-ehr tay-lay-foh-neek	phone book

août (m.) oo, oot	August
appeler ah-play	to call
apporter ah-pohr-tay	to bring (things)
apprendre ah-prahNdr	to learn
après ah-preh	after
après-midi (m.) ah-preh-mee-dee	afternoon
argent (m.) ahr-zhahN	money, silver
argent liquide (m.) ahr-zhahN lee-keed	cash
arrêt [m.] *d'autobus* ah-reh do-toh-bews	bus stop
arriver ah-ree-vay	to arrive
ascenseur (m.) ah-sahN-suhr	elevator
assez (de) ah-say (duh)	enough (of)
assiette (f.) ah-syeht	plate
attendre ah-tahNdr	to wait for
atterrir ah-tay-reer	to land
au lieu de o lyuh duh	instead of
au revoir o ruh-vwahr	goodbye
au-dessous de o duh-soo duh	below, beneath
au-dessus de o duh-sew duh	above
aujourd'hui o-zhoor-dwee	today

aussi o-see	also, too
automne (m.) o-tohn	autumn
autour de o-toor duh	around (surrounding)
autre otr	other
avance [f.] *de fonds* ah-vahNs duh fohN	cash advance
avant (de) ah-vahN (duh)	before
avion (m.) ah-vyohN	plane
avoir ah-vwahr	to have
avoir besoin de ah-vwahr buh-zwaN duh	to need
avoir chaud ah-vwahr sho	hot, to be hot (person)
avoir de la chance ah-vwahr duh lah shahNs	lucky, to be lucky
avoir faim ah-vwahr faN	hungry, to be hungry
avoir froid ah-vwahr frwah	cold, to be cold (person)
avoir hâte (de) ah-vwahr aht (duh)	hurry, to be in a hurry
avoir lieu ah-vwahr lyuh	to take place
avoir mal à ah-vwahr mahl	to have an ache (in)
avril (m.) ah-vreel	April
bain de bouche (m.) baN duh boosh	mouthwash
banque (f.) bahNk	bank
baskets (f. pl.) bahs-keht	sneakers

bateau (m.) bah-to	boat
berceau (m.) behr-so	crib
beurre (m.) buhr	butter
biberon (m.) bee-brohN	baby bottle
bibliothèque (f.) bee-blee-oh-tehk	library
bien byaN	well
bien sûr byaN sewr	of course
bientôt byaN-to	soon
bière (f.) byehr	beer
bijouterie (f.) bee-zhoo-tree	jewelry store
billet (m.) bee-yeh	bill (money), ticket
blanc(he) blahN (blahNsh)	white
bleu(e) bluh	blue
bœuf (m.) buhf	beef
boire bwahr	to drink
boîte (f.) bwaht	box, can
boîte [f.] *aux lettres* bwaht o lehtr	mailbox
bon(ne) bohN (bohn)	good
bonbons (m.) bohN-bohN	candy
bonjour bohN-zhoor	hello

bottes (f. pl.) boht	boots
bouche (f.) boosh	mouth
boucherie (f.) boosh-ree	butcher shop
boulangerie (f.) boo-lahN-zhree	bakery
bouteille (f.) boo-teh-y	bottle
boutique [f.] *de cadeaux* boo-teek duh kah-do	gift shop
bras (m.) brah	arm
brosse [f.] *à dents* brohs ah dahN	toothbrush
brun(e) bruhN (brewn)	brown
bureau (m.) bew-ro	office
bureau [m.] *de change* bew-ro duh shahNzh	money exchange
bureau [m.] *de tabac* bew-ro duh tah-bah	tobacco store
cabinet (m.) kah-bee-neh	office (medical)
café (m.) kah-fay	café, coffee
caissier (caissière) keh-syay (keh-syehr)	cashier
calculette (f.) kahl-kew-leht	calculator
carte (f.) kahrt	map, menu
carte [f.] *d'embarquement* kahrt dahN-bahrk-mahN	boarding pass
carte [f.] *de visite* kahrt duh vee-zeet	business card
carte postale (f.) kahrt pohs-tahl	postcard

carte téléphonique (f.) kahrt tay-lay-foh-neek	phone card
ceinture [f.] *de sécurité* saN-tewr duh say-kew-ree-tay	seat belt
célibataire say-lee-bah-tehr	single (unmarried)
cendrier (m.) sahN-dree-yay	ashtray
cent sahN	hundred
centre commercial (m.) sahNtr koh-mehr-syahl	mall
centre-ville (m.) sahNtr-veel	downtown
cerise (f.) suh-reez	cherry
chaise (f.) shehz	chair
chambre (f.) shahNbr	room
champignon (m.) shahN-pee-nyohN	mushroom
chapeau (m.) shah-po	hat
chaque shahk	each
chasseur (m.) shah-suhr	bellhop
chat (m.) shah	cat
chaussette (f.) sho-seht	sock
chaussure (f.) sho-sewr	shoe
chemise (f.) shuh-meez	shirt
chemisier (m.) shuh-mee-zyay	blouse
chèque (m.) shehk	check (money)

chercher shehr-shay	to look for
cheveux (m.) shuh-vuh	hair
chien (m.) shyaN	dog
cinéma (m.) see-nay-mah	movies, movie theater
cinq saNk	five
cinquante saN-kahNt	fifty
cintre (m.) saNtr	hanger
ciseaux (m. pl.) see-zo	scissors
citron (m.) see-trohN	lemon
clair(e) klehr	light (color)
clé (f.) klay	key
climatisation (f.) klee-mah-tee-zah-syohN	air conditioning
cœur (m.) kuhr	heart
coffre-fort (m.) kohfr-fohr	safe
combien kohN-byaN	how much, many
commander koh-mahN-day	to order
commencer koh-mahN-say	to begin
comment koh-mahN	how
commissariat [m.] *de police* koh-mee-sah-ryah duh poh-lees	police station
comprendre kohN-prahNdr	to understand

compris(e) kohN-pree(z)	included
confiserie (f.) kohN-feez-ree	candy store
confiture (f.) kohN-fee-tewr	jelly
conseiller kohN-say-yay	to advise, recommend
consulat américain (m.) kohN-sew-lah ah-may-ree-kaN	American consulate
contre kohNtr	against
couleur (f.) koo-luhr	color
court(e) koor(t)	short
couteau (m.) koo-to	knife
coûter koo-tay	to cost
couverture (f.) koo-vehr-tewr	blanket
covoiturage (m.) ko-vwah-tew-rahzh	rideshare
crayon (m.) kreh-yohN	pencil
crustacés (m. pl.) kroo-stah-say	seafood
cuillère (f.) kwee-yehr	spoon
cuir (m.) kweer	leather
cuisine (f.) kwee-zeen	kitchen, cooking
dans dahN	in
de duh	about, from, of
de rien duh ryaN	you're welcome

décembre (m.) day-sahNbr	December
décrire day-kreer	to describe
dedans duh-dahN	inside
dehors duh-ohr	outside
déjà day-zhah	already
demain duh-maN	tomorrow
demander duh-mahN-day	to ask
demi(e) duh-mee	half
dent (f.) dahN	tooth
dépenser day-pahN-say	to spend (money)
depuis duh-pwee	since (time)
dernier (dernière) dehr-nyay (dehr-nyehr)	last
derrière dehr-yehr	behind
désolé(e) day-zoh-lay	(I'm) sorry
dessous duh-soo	below, under
deux duh	two
devant duh-vahN	front, in front (of)
devoir duh-vwahr	to have to
dictionnaire (m.) deek-syoh-nehr	dictionary
difficile dee-fee-seel	difficult

dimanche (m.) dee-mahNsh	Sunday
dinde (f.) daNd	turkey
dire deer	to say, tell
disponible dees-poh-neebl	available
distributeur (m.) *de billets* dees-tree-bew-tuhr duh bee-yay	ATM
dix dees	ten
dix-huit dee-zweet	eighteen
dix-neuf deez-nuhf	nineteen
dix-sept dee-seht	seventeen
données (f. pl.) doh-nay	data
donner doh-nay	to give
douane (f.) dwahn	(border) customs
douleur (f.) doo-luhr	pain
doux (douce) doo(s)	sweet
douzaine (f.) doo-zehn	dozen
douze dooz	twelve
droit(e) drwah(t)	right (direction)
durer dew-ray	to last
eau (f.) o	water
eau minérale (f.) o mee-nay-rahl	mineral water

échanger ay-shahN-zhay	to exchange
échantillon (m.) ay-shahN-tee-yohN	sample
écouter ay-koo-tay	to listen to
écrire ay-kreer	to write
église (f.) ay-gleez	church
elle ehl	she
elles ehl	they (f.)
embarquer ahN-bahr-kay	to board
emprunter ahN-pruhN-tay	to borrow
en ahN	in
en face (de) ahN fahs (duh)	opposite, facing
en retard ahN ruh-tahr	late (in arriving)
en retraite ahN ruh-treht	retired
encore une fois ahN-kohr ewn fwah	again
entendre ahN-tahNdr	to hear
entre ahNtr	between
entrée (f.) ahN-tray	entrance
entretien (m.) ahNtr-tyaN	housekeeping service
envoyer ahN-vwah-yay	to send
épicé(e) ay-pee-say	spicy

épicerie (f.) ay-pees-ree	grocery store
escale (f.) ehs-kahl	stopover
espèces (f.) ehs-pehs	cash
espérer ehs-pay-ray	to hope
essayer ay-say-yay	to try, to try on
essence (f.) eh-sahNs	gasoline
est (m.) ehst	east
estomac (m.) ehs-toh-mah	stomach
étage (m.) ay-tahzh	floor (story)
États-Unis (m. pl.) ay-tah-zew-nee	United States
été (m.) ay-tay	summer
être ehtr	to be
étroit(e) ay-trwah(t)	narrow
expliquer ehks-plee-kay	to explain
face à fahs ah	in front of
facile fah-seel	easy
facture (f.) fahk-tewr	bill (commerce)
faire fehr	to do, make
faire chaud fehr sho	hot, to be hot (weather)
faire froid fehr frwah	cold, to be cold (weather)

famille (f.) fah-mee-y	family
femme (f.) fahm	wife
fermer fehr-may	to close
fête (f.) feht	holiday
février (m.) fay-vree-yay	February
fille (f.) fee-y	daughter
fils (m.) fees	son
finir fee-neer	to end, finish
foncé(e) fohN-say	dark (color)
fonctionner fohnk-syoh-nay	to work (function)
fourchette (f.) foor-sheht	fork
fraise (f.) frehz	strawberry
français (m.) frahN-seh	French (language)
français(e) frahN-seh(z)	French (nationality)
frère (m.) frehr	brother
fromage (m.) froh-mahzh	cheese
fruits [m. pl.] *de mer* frwee duh mehr	seafood
fumer few-may	to smoke
gagner gah-nyay	to earn, to win
gant (m.) gahN	glove

garder gahr-day	to keep
gare (f.) gahr	train station
gâteau (m.) gah-to	cake
gauche gosh	left (direction)
gérant(e) zhay-rahN(t)	manager
glace (f.) glahs	ice cream
glaçons (m. pl.) glah-sohN	ice cubes
gorge (f.) gohrzh	throat
grand magasin (m.) grahN mah-gah-zaN	department store
grand(e) grahNd	big, tall
gris(e) gree(z)	gray
heure (f.) uhr	hour, time
heureux (heureuse) uh-ruh (uh-ruhz)	happy
hier yehr	yesterday
hiver (m.) ee-vehr	winter
horloge (f.) ohr-lohzh	clock
huit weet	eight
ici ee-see	here
il eel	he
il y a eel yah	ago (+ time); there is, are

ils eel	they (m. or mixed-gender group)
impôt (m.) aN-po	tax
indépendant(e) aN-day-pahN-dahn(t)	self-employed
informations (f. pl.) aN-fohr-mah-syohN	news
interprète (m./f.) aN-tehr-preht	interpreter
jambe (f.) zhahNb	leg
jambon (m.) zhahN-bohN	ham
janvier (m.) zhahN-vyay	January
jaune zhon	yellow
je zhuh	I
jeudi (m.) zhuh-dee	Thursday
jeune zhuhn	young
joli(e) zhoh-lee	pretty
jouer zoo-ay	to play
jouir de zhoo-eer duh	to enjoy
jour (m.) zhoor	day
journal (m.) zhoor-nahl	newspaper
journée (f.) zhoor-nay	daytime
juillet (m.) zhwee-yeh	July
juin (m.) zhwaN	June

jupe (f.) zhewp	skirt
jus (m.) zhew	juice
jusqu'à zhew-skah	until
kiosk [m.] *à journaux* kee-ohsk ah zhoor-no	newsstand
laine (f.) lehn	wool
lait (m.) leh	milk
laitue (f.) lay-tew	lettuce
large lahrzh	wide
léger (légère) lay-zhay (lay-zhehr)	light (weight)
légume (m.) lay-gewm	vegetable
lentement lahNt-mahN	slowly
librairie (f.) lee-breh-ree	bookstore
lieu (m.) lyuh	place
ligne aérienne (f.) lee-nyuh ah-ay-ryehn	airline
lire leer	to read
livre (m.) leevr	book
livrer lee-vray	to deliver
loin (de) lwaN (duh)	far (from)
louer loo-ay	to rent
lundi (m.) luhN-dee	Monday

lunettes [f. pl.] *(de soleil)* lew-neht (duh soh-leh-y)	(sun)glasses
magasin (m.) mah-gah-zaN	store
magasin [f. pl.] *de chaussures* mah-gah-zaN duh sho-sewr	shoe store
magasin [f. pl.] *de souvenirs* mah-gah-zaN duh soov-neer	souvenir store
magasin [f. pl.] *de vêtements* mah-gah-zaN duh veht-mahN	clothing store
magasin de vins *et spiritueux* (m.) mah-gah-zaN duh vaN ay spee-ree-tew-uh	liquor store
mai (m.) meh	May
maillot de bain (m.) mah-yo duh baN	bathing suit
main (f.) maN	hand
maintenant maNt-nahN	now
maison (f.) meh-zohN	house
mal (adv.) mahl	bad
mal (f.) mahl	pain
malade mah-lahd	sick
manger mahN-zhay	to eat
maquillage (m.) mah-kee-yahzh	makeup
marché (m.) mahr-shay	market
mardi (m.) mahr-dee	Tuesday
mari (m.) mah-ree	husband

marié(e) mah-ryay	married
marron mah-rohN	brown
marque (f.) mahrk	brand name
mars (m.) mahrs	March
matin (m.) mah-taN	morning
mauvais(e) mo-veh(z)	bad
médecin mayd-saN	doctor
médicament (m.) may-dee-kah-mahN	medicine
mer (f.) mehr	sea
merci mehr-see	thank you
mercredi (m.) mehr-kruh-dee	Wednesday
mère (f.) mehr	mother
météo (f.) may-tay-o	weather forecast
métro (m.) may-tro	subway
mettre mehtr	to put
midi (m.) mee-dee	noon
mille meel	thousand
minuit (m.) mee-nwee	midnight
moins mwaN	less
mois (m.) mwah	month

moitié mwah-tyay	half
monnaie (f.) moh-neh	change (coins)
montre (f.) mohNtr	watch
montrer mohN-tray	to show
mot de passe (m.) mo duh pahs	password
mouchoir [m.] *en papier* moo-shwahr ahN pah-pyay	tissue
moutarde (f.) moo-tahrd	mustard
musée (m.) mew-zay	museum
neuf nuf	nine
noir(e) nwahr	black
nord (m.) nohr	north
note (f.) noht	bill (commerce)
nourriture (f.) noo-ree-tewr	food
nous noo	us, we
nouveau (nouvelle) noo-vo (noo-vehl)	new
novembre (m.) noh-vahNbr	November
numéro (m.) new-may-ro	number
numéro [m.] *de téléphone* new-may-ro duh tay-lay-fohn	phone number
octobre (m.) ohk-tohbr	October
œil (m. sing.), *yeux* (pl.) uh-y, yuh	eye

œuf (m.) uhf	egg
oignon (m.) oh-nyohN	onion
onze ohNz	eleven
or (m.) ohr	gold
ordinateur (m.) ohr-dee-nah-tuhr	computer
ordinateur portable (m.) ohr-dee-nah-tuhr pohr-tahbl	laptop
ordonnance (f.) ohr-doh-nahNs	prescription
oreille (f.) oh-reh-y	ear
oreiller (m.) oh-reh-yay	pillow
où oo	where
ouest (m.) wehst	west
ouvrir oo-vreer	to open
pain (m.) paN	bread
pansement (m.) pahNs-mahN	bandage
pansement adhésif (m.) pahNs-mahN ahd-ay-zeef	Band-Aid
pantalon (m.) pahN-tah-lohN	pants
papier (m.) pah-pyay	paper
paquet (m.) pah-keh	package
par pahr	by, through
parapluie (m.) pah-rah-plwee	umbrella

parce que pahrskuh	because
parler pahr-lay	to speak, talk
parmi pahr-mee	among
participer pahr-tee-see-pay	to participate
partir pahr-teer	to leave
pas de quoi pah duh kwah	you're welcome
passer pah-say	to spend (time)
pâté [m.] *de maison* pah-tay duh meh-zohN	block (street)
pâte [m.] *dentifrice* paht dahN-tee-frees	toothpaste
pauvre povr	poor
pays (m.) pay-ee	country
pendant pahN-dahN	during
perdre pehrdr	to lose
père (m.) pehr	father
petit(e) puh-tee(t)	small
petite cuillère (f.) puh-teet kwee-yehr	teaspoon
(un) peu (uhN) puh	(a) little
pied (m.) pyay	foot
pierre (f.) pyehr	stone
pilule (f.) pee-lewl	pill

piscine (f.) pee-seen	pool (swimming)
place (f.) plahs	seat
plage (f.) plahzh	beach
plus plew	more
poisson (m.) pwah-sohN	fish
poissonnerie (f.) pwah-sohn-ree	fish store
poivre (m.) pwahvr	pepper (seasoning)
pomme (f.) pohm	apple
pomme de terre (f.) pohm duh tehr	potato
portable (m.) pohr-tahbl	cell phone
porte (f.) pohrt	door (general), gate (airport)
portefeuille (m.) pohr-tuh-fuh-y	wallet
pot (m.) po	jar
poulet (m.) poo-leh	chicken
pour poor	for
pourboire (m.) poor-bwahr	tip (gratuity)
pourpre poor-pr	purple
pourquoi poor-kwah	why
pouvoir poo-vwahr	able (to be able), can
premier (*première*) pruh-myay (pruh-myehr)	first

prendre prahNdr	to take
près de preh duh	near (to)
presque prehsk	almost
prêter pray-tay	to lend
printemps (m.) praN-tahN	spring
prix (m.) pree	price
prochain(e) proh-shaN (-shehn)	next
propre prohpr	clean
puis pwee	then
quand kahN	when
quarante kah-rahNt	forty
quart (m.) kahr	quarter
quatorze kah-tohrz	fourteen
quatre kahtr	four
quatre-vingt-dix kahtr-vaN-dees	ninety
quatre-vingts kahtr-vaN	eighty
que kuh	what
quel(le) kehl	which
qui kee	who(m)
quinze kaNz	fifteen

quitter kee-tay	to leave
quoi kwah	what
recevoir ruh-suh-vwahr	to receive
recommander ruh-koh-mahN-day	to recommend
reçu (m.) ruh-sew	receipt
regarder ruh-gahr-day	to look at, watch
régler ray-glay	to adjust
remboursement (m.) rahN-boors-mahN	refund
remise (f.) ruh-meez	discount
rendez-vous (m.) rahN-day-voo	appointment, meeting
rendre rahNdr	to return (item)
rendre visite à rahNdr vee-zeet ah	to visit (person)
renseignements (m. pl.) rahN-seh-nyuh-mahN	information
rentrer rahN-tray	to return (go back)
réparer ray-pah-ray	to fix, repair
revue (f.) ruh-vew	magazine
rez-de-chaussée (m.) rayd sho-say	ground floor
rhume (m.) rewm	cold (illness)
riz (m.) ree	rice
robe (f.) rohb	dress

rose roz	pink
rouge roozh	red
rue (f.) rew	street
s'il vous plaît seel voo pleh	please
sac (m.) sahk	bag, pocketbook, purse
sale sahl	dirty
salle (f.) sahl	room
salle [f.] *de bains* sahl duh baN	bathroom
salle [f.] *de gym* sahl duh zheem	fitness center
samedi (m.) sahm-dee	Saturday
sans sahN	without
seize sehz	sixteen
sel (m.) sehl	salt
semaine (f.) suh-mehn	week
sept seht	seven
septembre (m.) sehp-tahNbr	September
serviette (f.) sehr-vyeht	napkin, towel
signifier see-nee-fyay	to mean
six sees	six
sœur (f.) suhr	sister

soie (f.) swah	silk
soir (m.) swahr	evening
soixante swah-sahNt	sixty
soixante-dix swah-sahNt-dees	seventy
sortie (f.) sohr-tee	exit
sortir sohr-teer	to go out
soucoupe (f.) soo-koop	saucer
soulier (m.) soo-lyay	shoe
sous soo	under
souvent soo-vahN	often
stade (m.) stahd	stadium
stylo-bille (m.) stee-lo-bee-y	ballpoint pen
sucre (m.) sewkr	sugar
sud (m.) sewd	south
suivre sweevr	to follow
supermarché (m.) sew-pehr-mahr-shay	supermarket
sur sewr	on, upon
sympathique saN-pah-teek	nice
tard tahr	late (in the day)
tarif (m.) tah-reef	fare

tasse (f.) tahs	cup
taux de change (m.) to duh shahNzh	exchange rate
temps (m.) tahN	weather, time
tennis (m. pl.) tay-nees	sneakers
terminer tehr-mee-nay	to end
tête (f.) teht	head
thé (m.) tay	tea
timbre (m.) taNbr	stamp (mail)
tôt to	early
toucher (un chèque) too-shay (uhN shehk)	to cash (a check)
toujours too-zhoor	always, still
tout (toute, tous, toutes) too (toot, too, toot)	all
travailler trah-vah-yay	to work (employment)
treize trehz	thirteen
trente trahNt	thirty
très treh	very
trois trwah	three
trop tro	too much
trouver troo-vay	to find
tu tew	you

un(e) uhN (ewn)	one
végétalien(ne) vay-zhay-tah-lyaN (-lyehn)	vegan
végétarien(ne) vay-zhay-tah-ryaN (-ryehn)	vegetarian
vendeur (vendeuse) vahN-duhr (vahN-duhz)	salesperson
vendre vahNdr	to sell
vendredi (m.) vahN-druh-dee	Friday
venir vuh-neer	to come
ventre (m.) vahNtr	stomach
verre (m.) vehr	glass
vert(e) vehr(t)	green
veste (f.) vehst	jacket
veuve (veuf) vuhv (vuhf)	widow(er)
viande (f.) vyahNd	meat
vieux (vieil, vieille) vyuh (vyay, vyay)	old
vin (m.) vaN	wine
vingt vaN	twenty
vite veet	quickly
vitre (f.) veetr	window (car)
vivre veevr	to live
voir vwahr	to see

voiture (f.) vwah-tewr	car
vol (m.) vohl	flight
vouloir voo-lwahr	to want
vous voo	you

Index